Achieving Inventory Accuracy

A Guide to Sustainable
Class A Excellence in 120 Days

BY
DONALD H. SHELDON
CFPIM, CIRM

THE EDUCATIONAL SOCIETY
FOR RESOURCE MANAGEMENT

Copyright ©2004 by J. Ross Publishing, Inc.

ISBN 1-932159-31-2

Printed and bound in the U.S.A. Printed on acid-free paper
10 9 8 7 6 5 4 3 2 1

Library of Congress Cataloging-in-Publication Data

Sheldon, Donald H.
  Achieving inventory accuracy : a guide to sustainable class a
excellence in 120 days / by Donald H. Sheldon.
       p. cm.
  Includes index.
  ISBN 1-932159-31-2 (hardcover : alk. paper)
  1. Inventory control. I. Title.
  TS160.S515 2004
  658.7'87—dc22   2004005588

Phone: (561) 869-3900
Fax: (561) 892-0700
Web: www.jrosspub.com

Table of Contents

Dedication

Special love and thanks to
Anita, Erica, and Geoff
for their patience and support
and to God for his blessings.

Preface

It is curious…evidence suggests that more than 50 percent of North American businesses allow their inventory record accuracy to flounder below acceptable, cost-effective levels. Using the world as a base, accuracy habits are even worse. The ironic part about inventory inaccuracy is that it is one of the easiest process improvements to accomplish when the right process steps are implemented. It is also one of the more effective methods to aid in minimizing unnecessary costs.

The good news is that a robust inventory accuracy control process is not technology dependent. It is also not expensive or capital dependent and the effort will always produce returns far greater than the normal justification threshold for project expenditures. Neither bar code technology nor steel fencing will make accuracy a reality. Inventory record accuracy is simply a process control with the focus on consistency and discipline. It is easy to achieve and many businesses have proven it.

Organizations like Buker, Inc., from which I received my initial consulting exposure to the world's manufacturing, and like DHSheldon & Associates, where my experience continues, have worked with thousands of organizations all over the world. This experience has allowed the realization of common denominators and proven steps, the best of which have always (yes, always) resulted in predictable successful data accuracy. If the steps in this book are implemented conscientiously, the result will be sustainable, high levels of accuracy — every time!

This book is a summarization of my experiences, from both employers and clients. The objective of this text is to outline the steps required to achieve sustainable, high levels of inventory record accuracy. The result is a step-by-step, day-by-day approach that, when followed, will reduce dramatically the variability and cost caused by inaccurate inventory balance data. It can be expected that these steps will give you the same results numerous others have seen before.

About the Author

 **Donald H. Sheldon** is President of the DHSheldon & Associates consulting firm in New York. He started his career at The Raymond Corporation, a world-class manufacturer of material handling equipment. He held the position of Director and General Manager of Raymond's Worldwide Aftermarket Services Division when he left to accept the position of Vice President for Buker, Inc., of Chicago, a globally recognized leader in management education and consulting. While at Buker, Mr. Sheldon helped clients on every continent to achieve business excellence in numerous areas including inventory accuracy. After several years of traveling with Buker, Mr. Sheldon joined NCR Corporation, a client company, to work full time with its manufacturing facilities throughout Asia, Northern Africa, Europe, and the Americas. As Vice President of Global Quality and Six Sigma Services, Mr. Sheldon was directly involved in the process improvement health worldwide at NCR. In 2003, Mr. Sheldon, to continue to support his passion for coaching excellence, launched DHSheldon & Associates. He and his network of consultants continue to work with companies in North America to improve competitive advantage.

Mr. Sheldon has published numerous articles in journals and is co-author (with Michael Tincher) of the book *The Road to Class A Manufacturing Resource Planning (MPR II)*, published in 1995 and available at www.amazon.com. He has been a frequent speaker at colleges, international conventions, and seminars including APICS (American Production and Inventory Control Society). He holds a Master of Arts Degree in Business and Government Policies Studies and an undergraduate degree in Business and Economics both from the State University of New York, Empire State College. He is certified by APICS as CFPIM (Certified Fellow in Production and Inventory Management) and as CIRM (Certified in Resource Management).

Mr. Sheldon can be contacted at www.sheldoninc.com.

Acknowledgments

Many experienced and knowledgeable people influenced and helped put this book together. The vast experiences of manufacturing veterans including the following have given great help over the years:

- Mike Tincher, friend and President of Buker, Inc. and author of *High Velocity Manufacturing* (Buker, 1995) and co-author (with me) of *The Road to Class A Manufacturing Resource Planning (MRP II)* (Buker, 1995).
- Bob Wilkins, long-time friend and Director, Quality & Kaizen, Veeco Instruments and author of *The Quality Empowered Business* (Prentice Hall, 1994).
- Mike Stickler, friend and President of Empowered Performance, LLC.
- Paul Potter, friend and Executive Vice President of Buker, Inc. and author of *Inventory Record Accuracy Guaranteed!* (Buker, 2003).

These gentlemen have had an impact in my learning over the years, especially in the beginning of my consulting career, and I am grateful. Without their help, this book would not be a reality.

About APICS

APICS — The Educational Society for Resource Management is a not-for-profit international educational organization recognized as the global leader and premier provider of resource management education and information. APICS is respected throughout the world for its education and professional certification programs. With more than 60,000 individual and corporate members in 20,000 companies worldwide, APICS is dedicated to providing education to improve an organization's bottom line. No matter what your title or need, by tapping into the APICS community you will find the education necessary for success.

APICS is recognized globally as:

- The source of knowledge and expertise for manufacturing and service industries across the entire supply chain
- The leading provider of high-quality, cutting-edge educational programs that advance organizational success in a changing, competitive marketplace
- A successful developer of two internationally recognized certification programs, Certified in Production and Inventory Management (CPIM) and Certified in Integrated Resource Management (CIRM)
- A source of solutions, support, and networking for manufacturing and service professionals

For more information about APICS programs, services, or membership, visit www.apics.org or contact APICS Customer Support at (800) 444-2742 or (703) 354-8851.

Free value-added materials available from
the Download Resource Center at www.jrosspub.com

At J. Ross Publishing we are committed to providing today's professional with practical, hands-on tools that enhance the learning experience and give readers an opportunity to apply what they have learned. That is why we offer free ancillary materials available for download on this book and all participating Web Added Value™ publications. These online resources may include interactive versions of material that appears in the book or supplemental templates, worksheets, models, plans, case studies, proposals, spreadsheets and assessment tools, among other things. Whenever you see the WAV™ symbol in any of our publications, it means bonus materials accompany the book and are available from the Web Added Value Download Resource Center at www.jrosspub.com.

Downloads available for *Achieving Inventory Accuracy: A Guide to Sustainable Class A Excellence in 120 Days* consist of slides covering Class A excellence in inventory accuracy and steps to achieving world-class performance including Class A ERP, best-in-class lean, and customer-focused quality (Six Sigma).

1

Understanding Data Integrity

It is amazing. Despite the fact that inventory accuracy is so easy to obtain and cost effective, it still eludes many manufacturing and service organizations. Even many of the larger companies still have data integrity issues that create unnecessary variation in their planning and manufacturing processes. The tragedy is the simplicity of the issue. It is really just a matter of management expectation.

Introduction

Inventory inaccuracy is a curable cancer that plagues more than half of the world's businesses. "Inaccuracy," as we will use it, refers to less-than-adequate process control over inventory piece-part location balance records. Accuracy is measured as physical quantity compared to the computer "perpetual" record where accuracy is only exact matches. The generally accepted minimum threshold of acceptability for inventory record accuracy is 95 percent in high-performance businesses. In other words, for every one hundred inventory balance records, ninety-five must be perfect.

When offsetting variation such as from currency-based metrics is used, accuracy is not posted accurately. The minuses offset the positive variances.

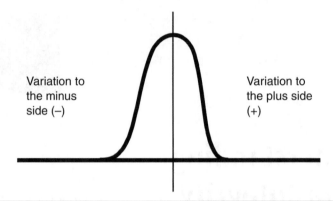

Figure 1-1. Variation curve for inventory inaccuracies.

Many organizations do not even track their accuracy on a day-to-day basis. These companies determine accuracy by the costly physical wall-to-wall inventory they take periodically, usually only once a year. When a periodic inventory is used, it is often to validate the company's valuation of inventory on its financial statements. Inventory accuracy must not be determined by currency valuations alone.

The laws of statistics remind us that in any random distribution of data, there will be an equal number of data points on the minus side of the bell curve as will be on the plus side when looking at inventory balance accuracy (see Figure 1-1). When currency is used, these data points offset each other, resulting in a false sense of accuracy. Every balance *could* be inaccurate, but the netting effect could and would probably show accuracy to be very close to perfect — often 99 percent or better. When piece-part balances are used in those same organizations and location balances compared, the true accuracy levels are exposed. The resulting measurement and performance understanding is much different. It often is a real eye opener!

Production planning systems use inventory balances, not the currency values, to support item planning. For this reason, it becomes important to seek high levels of process control at the item-quantity detail level.

Achieving inventory record accuracy requires a cultural shift in most organizations. The way organizations think and work has to change. The result of this change is usually a massive reduction (50 percent or more) in inventory that previously was needed to buffer the inaccurate item balances. In every organization

Every organization that has implemented the steps outlined in this book has seen great benefits.

that has implemented the steps as outlined in this book, the results have included significant savings in overhead and inventory costs.

These savings come from reduced expediting, reduced priority freight, reduced overtime, smoother work flows, less inventory carrying costs, and higher customer service levels. And it is easy to do. Achieving inventory record accuracy is a matter of expectation!

Look at the banking business, for example. In every aspect of currency control, there are very high levels of inventory accuracy. Banks have such high accuracy levels that we as consumers come to expect it. Some warehouse managers have suggested that there is an association between pay scale and accuracy expectations and that low pay scales of stock pickers and material handlers are often at the core of data integrity issues. The bank model does not seem to prove that statement out. Most bank tellers get pretty modest pay. The difference is expectation. When they do not balance at the end of the day, the tellers may be required to stay and reconcile. Do the storeroom clerks in your business do that? Most likely they do not. Obviously, it is more sophisticated than simply expecting results and staying late to achieve them. It has a lot to do with understanding the processes and establishing controls on these processes. *It must be easier to do it right than to do it wrong!*

> It must be easier to do it right than to do it wrong!

In the case of a manufacturing organization, raw material typically flows through a process while it is converted into finished goods that either ship directly to a customer, ship into distribution, or go into a storage area in anticipation of an order. In every area where inventory is "staged" for more than a few hours, some accounting of the inventory might take place. In many manufacturing organizations, this means that raw material balances, work-in-process balances, and/or finished goods inventory balances exist. Transactions typically happen at these "staging" points. Having high expectations and standards for transaction accuracy and robust process control is the only answer for predictability in the outcomes of these transactions. Just like the banking sector that understands and acknowledges its transaction points and inventory staging, the manufacturing organization needs to have process controls designed, procedures in place, people trained, results measured, *and* high expectations. The result is high levels of predictability, lower costs, and higher customer service.

It is not much different in a service company such as an airline. In an airline business, many service items and parts are kept on hand for quick availability during unscheduled or scheduled maintenance. Some wearable parts may even be stored in locations all over the globe. The issues in the service sector are similar to the manufacturing concerns. In every location where inventory is staged, for each inventory movement, a transaction needs to be recorded. The alternative is uncertainty or variability added to the process and data integrity jeopardized.

One airline, for example, had a general disregard for inventory transaction disciplines. This same airline also had (and has) a flawless safety record and respected its procedures for maintenance and repair with all the enthusiasm you would want from a company that was going to carry you 35,000 feet off the ground! For some reason, the expectations were not as high when it came to inventory transactions. Airlines understand process control. These people immediately acknowledge the importance of creating predictable results. They understand this very well from their maintenance procedures. They simply had not associated the same level of discipline with inventory balance accuracy. Again, it is a matter of expectation.

Inventory is a dirty word in most organizations. Once you have "been to the seminar" and/or "read the book," you quickly become a disciple for the **no inventory** program. That is a fallacy in many manufacturing and service organizations. Most inventory in the majority of manufacturing or service companies is positioned to offset variation in their processes. Some of the sources for variation include:

- Demand forecast inaccuracies
- Scrap reporting errors or omissions
- Inconsistencies in amounts produced as compared to requested
- Normal (ill-behaved) customers
- Machine downtime
- Yield rates
- etc.

One of the ironic sources for variation is the inventory accuracy itself. When there is lack of inventory balance accuracy, planners resolved to "survival mode" will position offsetting inventory buffers to allow higher service levels. It does not take inventory planners very long to learn this lesson. It only takes getting "stung" by a missing component a couple of times before the planner will compensate by adding buffer to the next order and the cycle begins. This is

When inventory data are inaccurate, the planners resort to "survival mode."

often in direct conflict with management goals for inventory management, but because the highest priority is to serve customers appropriately, the practice flourishes. This is how "tribal knowledge" influences a company's culture. Because the behavior works, it becomes accepted and the norm.

Lower inventory is often a priority with top management in many businesses. When the business goal of lower inventory periodically is brought to the top of the priority list, the materials people get excited

> **W**hen management asks to have inventory lowered, planners can only affect the (needed) new inventory they order. The other inventory is already there.

about the cause and, not surprisingly, inventory goes down. While lowering inventory, there is only one area planners can really help quickly — they can influence levels of new material they order. This same inventory is (hopefully) the component inventory required by customer requirements. When an inventory reduction focus simply is forced on the planners, the result, many times, is increased shortages with no corresponding decrease in process variation. The organization still has the wrong "stuff" inflating inventory

> **I**nventory record accuracy is an important source of process variation and one that can be conquered.

dollar values. The shortage and expedite mode that follows translates into self-induced burden cost. The root cause of the problem is often not the buffer itself; it is the inaccuracy leading to the buffers.

The first step in limiting inventory investment should be to eliminate as much variability in the process as possible, thereby eliminating the *need* for the inventory. Inventory record accuracy is one important source of variation, many times the easiest and quickest to eliminate.

Is Inventory Really a Bad Thing?

Inventory is not a bad thing. The books are wrong! Let me prove it to you. I am not a mechanic, but I like to think about being one once in a while. I have always dreamed of a garage with a lot of tools and the infamous "red toolboxes." You know the kind, the ones that stack and make you look like a mechanic who knows what he or she is doing. A couple of years ago, I finally reached the age when it was time to go and get them for my garage. My son, Geoff, went with me because he understands the need for red toolboxes. We were going to have a fun day!

We went to the local hardware store, one of those chain warehouse types with a lot of choices. The red toolbox aisle had at least twenty different configurations, options, and features to choose from. After about thirty or forty minutes, Geoff and I had picked out three different sections we wanted that would make our setup perfect. We were excited about leaving money at this store and taking the red toolboxes home. We pulled the tickets and took them to the cashier.

After handing the tickets in and smiling to the cashier, he responded, "I need to check inventory." That seemed like a reasonable next step to me. The check on the first section came up with an inventory balance of three. "Good," I said. "Not good," he replied. "That means we probably don't have any." (My son knows what I do for a living and started to see humor in this that I was not experiencing.)

"Good," I said. "Not good," he replied. "That means we probably don't have any."

After two more checks and a physical check of inventory, we were disappointed. Inventory would have been a good thing for this merchant that afternoon. It always is when the customer is ready to convert it into cash. From this point forward, please think of inventory as a good thing. The best companies have exactly what customers want, when they want it. Organizations that do not have controls over their data accuracy will not be successful in the long term and will certainly be at a disadvantage compared to competitors that have concentrated in this space. There is no more important and yet simple effort a company can make.

2

Building the Case for Data Accuracy as a Prerequisite to High Performance

Data are an important asset in every business. They are as important as the inventory itself, and when the concepts are combined (INVENTORY DATA), we suddenly realize that we are entrusted with some very valuable assets. High-performance organizations treat inventory record accuracy accordingly.

In both manufacturing and service organizations, inventory accuracy is linked directly to the ability to service customers adequately. Nothing is more frustrating than ordering a consumer product that is available at order entry but backordered in shipping due to warehouse balance errors. Inventory accuracy processes in manufacturing organizations not only affect the customer, but can also add expense as employees become nonproductive as a result of surprise shortages. In both make-to-stock and make-to-order environments with inaccurate inventory records, surprise shortages can often result in business lost to competition. In the rare instance when the customer is

Any way you slice it, inventory inaccuracy costs you money.

patient, surprises cause unscheduled equipment and tooling changeovers and interruptions in what might otherwise be a smooth-flowing and more cost-effective operation. Any way you slice it, inventory record inaccuracy costs money.

Costs of Inaccurate Inventory Balances

Inventory accuracy costs more than many management teams realize. This is evidenced by the hundreds of organizations that still today do not have at least 95 percent accuracy. Let's look at some of these cost factors that can affect any business.

- **Replenishment costs** — When balances are not accurate, surprises cause additional orders to be placed "on rush." Other times, orders are reduced or "partialed" to complete production operations and receive inventory to stock earlier than planned due to a surprise. This results in additional orders and increased replenishment costs even when the inventory causing the shortage is very inexpensive. Orders can increase costs of office transactions in accounting and purchasing by significant amounts for every additional purchase order or release that is made. Add the additional factory and warehouse transactions that can happen in some companies and you are talking real money.
- **Carrying costs** — Inventory levels are a result of need caused by uncertainty. This uncertainty *can* be caused by volatility in customer demand patterns, but it can also be and often is a factor caused by inventory balance inaccuracy. When there is a possibility of running out of product or inventory because of surprises in data, more inventory is required to offset the variability. Money tied up in stagnant inventory is money not available for other business investments and improvements. The costs are more than simply the cost of money. Opportunity costs must be considered.
- **Obsolescence** — Any time that inventory sits around for very long, it can be revised by new technology or become obsolete due to changing markets. In the electronics market, for example, product life cycles are so short that obsolescence is planned into every cycle, which can happen several times a year. Having inaccurate data and inflated buffers to cover the variation increases the risk of waste.

■ **Orphaned inventory** — Related to the topic of revised designs, when product phaseouts of preceding designs occur within new product introductions, data accuracy issues make it virtually impossible to synchronize the phaseout of all on-hand inventory. The result is increased risk of waste.

■ **Stockout costs** — Surprise stockouts contribute to a variety of cost increases. Before listing some of them, remember that if there is a history of such surprises, there will be a tendency to staff for the resulting mad scrambles. Stockout costs need to start with overstaffing. The first thought of increases in cost from stockouts usually includes nonproductive time in production, priority freight costs, expediting resources, overtime, etc. Surprise stockouts are never a welcome event in a customer service or market-driven organization. Lost sales are a difficult risk to put a monetary value on, but we all understand the impact and risk.

■ **Other capacity-related costs** — When surprise shortages are experienced frequently, nonlinear production schedules usually result. In many businesses, this might mean excessive overtime, especially at the end of the month. The best utilization of the production workforce is a relatively even, predictable workload. Any surprises that can be eliminated reduce cost. Inventory inaccuracy is one of the easier surprise sources to eliminate.

■ **Control system costs** — Surprise shortages are a hindrance to everyone. When a particular critical component is unexpectedly on shortage more than once, extra caution is often administered using activities such as frequent balance checks or cycle counts, informal systems created using logs outside the formal system, and extra expediting staff to offset this variability. Obviously, all of these commonly executed control system buffers cost the business money and work against competitive advantage.

There are other cost risks, but the above list should be enough to get you and your management staff behind this valuable effort.

Material Requirements Planning

Although enterprise resource planning (ERP) software suppliers do not like to admit it, almost all high-performance manufacturing organizations still utilize material requirements planning (MRP) in their inventory planning process. MRP is a computer-driven requirements-calculating program found in virtually all ERP business systems, old and new.

In newer systems it may be called something else (such as advanced scheduling), but the inner workings revolve around a calculation that nets planned and possessed inventory against planned and actual requirements. The MRP program takes data from the customer requirement or forecast schedule and other sources within the business system software and nets on-hand inventory balances and on-order or planned inventory quantities to schedule component requirement dates.

In most manufacturing organizations, this MRP calculation is the process tool that creates the communicated signal or message used by planners to order or reschedule inventory to meet planned and firm requirements, especially out beyond a firm fence. This information is very helpful to the supply base. The more accurate it is, the easier it is to manage cost out of the supply chain.

There are other important inputs to MRP as well. Customer orders or stock replenishment requirements at the top planning level, in high-performance organizations, are aligned by capacity, a process often referred to as master scheduling or master production scheduling (MPS). Master scheduling is the process of scheduling customer demand and forecast requirements into realistic production or process schedules. The resulting established requirement dates are a critical input to the MRP accuracy in ordering the right inventory. Again, the common theme — accuracy of inventory has a major impact on all of these system elements.

Enterprise Resource Planning

The American Production and Inventory Control Society (APICS) defines ERP in two widely accepted approaches:

1. ERP is a software system.
2. ERP is a business process.

ERP is a business system that links the processes from top management planning to schedule execution tightly together. It is not just software to help facilitate and manage it.

Much confusion was developed by ERP software sellers who advertised and marketed their wares as the answer to manufacturing advantage. This led to the definition of ERP as a software tool. For the purposes of this book, the assumption

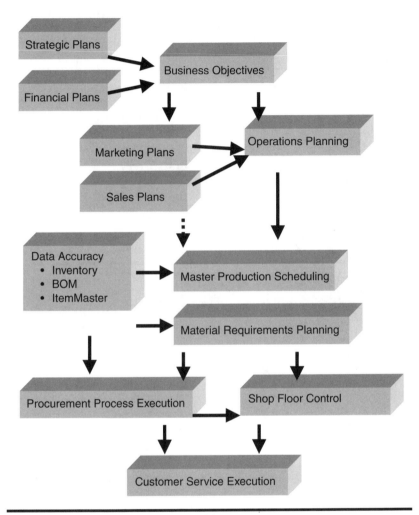

Figure 2-1. ERP business system model.

is made that ERP is a business process and that ERP software is a tool to help with the efficient execution of this business process.

An ERP business model was adopted by many high-performance organizations in the 1990s. Different models vary, but most basically are similar in design to the process schematic illustrated in Figure 2-1.

The model ascribes to certain expectations, from top management through to execution of schedules and maintenance of data. In high-performance organizations utilizing ERP, MPS and MRP are two important planning and scheduling processes with specific expected process

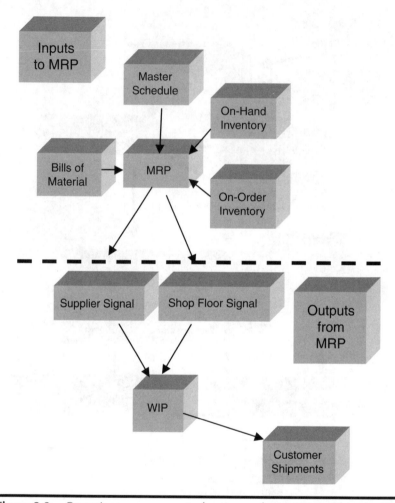

Figure 2-2.   Operations management planning and execution within the ERP business model.

controls. Neither of these processes can work effectively without accurate data. In Figure 2-2, MRP is the focus, showing the inputs utilized within the program.

Figure 2-2 illustrates the relationship and dependencies created by the MRP business system. As variation such as inaccurate on-hand inventory is introduced, there is a direct linkage to declining customer service and/ or increased cost. The signals or outputs from MRP to suppliers and to the shop floor only become more and more inaccurate.

If, for example, in the preceding model, there were inaccuracies in the inventory balances as an input to the planning process, the output would be affected negatively. Planners would either have to have additional inventory to offset the variation or they would expedite surprise shortages regularly. Some companies even have their organizational structure designed to specialize in a reactionary type of process. This normally means they have extra capacity for effective expediting. Either way, costs are increased unnecessarily.

Class A ERP

In the 1980s, as interest in reducing cost continued to expand, many high-performance organizations interested in optimizing the flow of information and material through the supply chain adopted specific levels of performance as their goal. Started initially by Oli Wight, in some circles these goals were adapted into an accepted standard called Class A MRP II (manufacturing resource planning). Later, as MRP II expanded its depth of process into customer and supplier linkages, it was referred to as ERP. *Class A* MRP II expanded as well and evolved into *Class A* ERP.

Class A ERP is a standard used for businesses achieving the high-performance levels of ERP performance. If you have never heard the term Class A ERP, do not feel alone. Although very successful where adopted, the performance standard called "Class A ERP" was limited in its worldwide acceptance.

Much of the early ERP market-speak was derived from software marketing hype. Some believe that the ERP software companies saw the Class A model as counterproductive to selling software and therefore not on their agenda. Instead, it was more beneficial to promote their wares as the entire answer. Many companies looked at this favorably because "plug and play" seemed a lot easier than all the work and discipline that process improvement seemed to require. The more the software companies marketed this thinking, the more the mainstream opinion shifted toward defining ERP as software. As mentioned, even APICS identifies ERP with two definitions now: software and the process itself. This is a good example of culture changing the language. Purists like myself may never get used to accepting the software angle!

The Class A ERP process tends to focus on the process and not as much on the software tools. Class A criteria are worth a second look; let's define Class A performance.

Class A ERP organizations can be characterized as having well-established planning processes and predictability in their business flow. The performance designation sometimes certified by outside consultants started in manufacturing, but can apply to almost all businesses today: distribution, manufacturing, remanufacturing, as well as the service sector. The required threshold of acceptability for Class A ERP status in selected areas includes:

> **C**lass A is worth a second look when creating a continuous improvement management system.

- Bill of material accuracy, 99 percent
- Master schedule accuracy, 95 percent
- Inventory location balance accuracy, 95 percent

Later in this book, the actual proscribed methods for measuring these processes will be discussed. There are a number of consulting organizations in the world that certify Class A performance. My organization, DHSheldon & Associates (www.sheldoninc.com), is one such consulting business that subscribes to the Class A model. Our approach in the Class A ERP space uses five areas of Class A ERP certification performance criteria:

1. Prioritization and management of business objectives
   - Project management
   - Human capital management and investment
   - Business imperatives
2. Sales and Operations Planning processes
3. Scheduling disciplines and production planning
4. Data integrity
5. Execution of schedules and plans

During ERP implementations, process improvements in all five areas result in the elimination of variation affecting predictability of process and, ultimately, process control. Obviously, inventory accuracy plays an important part in Class A ERP certification and high operating performance achievement.

3

Day 1–3: Preparing for Inventory Record Accuracy

Preparing for Day 1: Education and establishing accountability.

Day 1: Kickoff. Management should announce to all employees involved that it is in support of the effort and that it WILL BE SUCCESSFUL! This is also a good time to introduce the process owners to the group. An overview of what the process focus will entail is appropriate in this first session.

Days 2–3: Education continues

There is one step that carries little controversy among successful organizations that have achieved inventory location balance accuracy. That step is education and training. It is education that enables the masses, and therefore it is the first and most important step. Training keeps everyone in sync.

If a manager gives an employee a directive, as long as it clears the minimal acceptable standards set by ethical, legal, and moral filters, the action is usually carried out. If this management request involves a change in practice and works against well-established organizational habits, the directive may be carried out initially, but may not be effective in changing ongoing habits! Humans hate change. It seems to be a given trait. But what if the employees understand "why" the directive was given and have a grasp on what's in it for them? At that point, the employees stand a much better chance of being excited about the new change and willing to participate in a new way of doing things. Education can enable that understanding, willingness, and excitement. Education is the main way to affect culture in an organization. If it is followed up by management showing support and willingness to walk the talk, the prescription for success usually is quite predictably favorable. This sets the stage for the first day.

> **E**mployees want to know what's in it for them. Management needs to communicate the answer.

Morning of Day 1: First Event/Kickoff

Education should begin with the entire organization involved right away with inventory transactions and flow. The first educational step should be an introduction from management to establish the priority and expectations going forward for inventory record accuracy.

On the first day, management should hold an event or kickoff to emphasize its priority on the topic of inventory record accuracy. This means that the top-ranking manager in the facility leads the discussion. Obviously, this manager needs to be versed in the expectations and be able to articulate them at this gathering — set the stage for expectations, communicate the objectives, establish the time frames, and anoint the team leaders. The excitement level at this meeting should be high to send the message of prioritization of this effort.

One manager in Holyoke, Massachusetts, had all of the warehouse team sign a football at this meeting. He declared that the touchdown scored by achieving 95 percent inventory balance accuracy would go a long way to help the entire company win the Super Bowl, which was how he described becoming the low-cost producer in their market. This was very effective packaging. It added a flavor of excitement that kept the attention of the attendees. Fewer words were missed and the point was made effectively. You can come up with your own spin. Inventory accuracy is fun, so have fun with it.

Afternoon of Day 1: Creating the Task Team

Most successful data accuracy implementations start by naming a task team to own the process and lead the charge of inventory record accuracy. These task teams are normally and ideally made up of between three and seven team members and should not be led by, but should be sponsored directly by, the highest manager in operations for the particular facility implementation. In addition to the team members, there will be team leaders and support people assigned. These support people will work with the team as required, but will not necessarily be full-time members. Members and support personnel could logically include:

- The warehouse manager (team leader)
- Two of the most conscientious warehouse employees (members)
- Representation from the materials department (member or support)
- Representation from information technology (support)
- Representation from finance (support)
- Supervisors in departments with "point-of-use" storage inventory (member or support)

The team design should clarify member roles (see Figure 3-1). For example, the core team is accountable for the ultimate achievement of goals. Other support members such as information technology or materials may or may not be full-time members depending on the organizational needs. It is especially effective if the sponsor is the top management in operations, normally with the warehouse manager leading the team and acting as process owner for inventory accuracy. I make the assumption in this statement that the warehouse manager reports to this sponsor. In some organizations, the materials manager might also be involved as the sponsor. Top management would still be involved. Some groups have developed a steering committee to engage them. Just make sure they are part of the process. These roles are important.

> Just make sure top management is part of the process in some way, either as a sponsor or in the role of steering committee to review progress. They can carry water as necessary — lots of it!

It is up to the management champion of the inventory accuracy initiative (the top operations manager in the facility) to charge the group

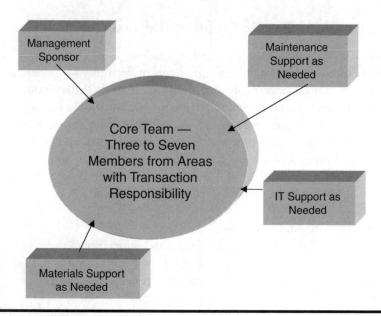

Figure 3-1. Team structure.

with its problem statement or task. During the launch of the team, management should communicate the following.

Determine the Objective

Management has a responsibility to define the expected outcome of the task team's efforts clearly. Inventory accuracy is easy to define in the first wave. "Inventory location balances within all warehouse, stores, and point-of-use areas will be at a minimum level of accuracy of 95 percent in 120 days (date). The measurement will be the percentage of perfect location balances with applied tolerances of A ±0 percent, B ±2 percent, and C ±3 percent (see Chapter 11 on performance measurement) as compared to the location balances checked."

There will be questions at the session about the measurement process. Save these questions for the next day and a half of education.

Choose the Team

The typical team makeup has been described earlier, but it should be clear that the team can bring in resources as needed during the duration of the project. These resources might include manufacturing engineers for storage layout issues, the materials people for demand information as needed, etc. The project champion or sponsor (operations manager) should be contacted by the task team leader if and when any barriers are encountered due to prioritization of resource.

Determine the Time Frame to Reach the Objective

The objective is achievable in 120 days. To prolong it is to waste precious time unnecessarily. By following the steps in this book day by day and keeping the resources and attention on it, inventory record accuracy should be achievable and maintained in 120 days. It is important to note that this process improvement has taken longer at many, many organizations. The truth is, however, that as soon as a team gets serious — really serious — it only takes about 120 days. Organizations that plan longer process implementations never take less time.

Choose the Team Leader

The manager responsible for the most inventory locations in the facility is a good candidate to be the task team (or project team) leader. This could be the warehouse or inventory control manager or could even be the production manager if there are a lot of point-of-use inventory locations. The task can and should be divided into segments for focus, but the overall process ownership should reside with one individual as there are transaction decisions required that affect all areas and software decisions that should be consistent facility-wide. Accountability in this sense is the functionality to oversee the successful implementation, ensure consistency of process, be the tie-breaker in problem resolution, gather metrics from various stores areas, and report to management or the steering committee.

Determine the Team Champion or Sponsor

Management needs to be involved if a sustainable process is to be accomplished in the 120-day time frame. A higher level management resource such as the plant manager, material manager, or operations manager or director should be assigned to the inventory accuracy team. This manager's responsibility is to ensure the success of the team. If the team members need education, if they need engineering help, if maintenance is required, management has the responsibility to guide them and "carry water" for them when necessary.

Obviously, the team leader also needs to report directly to this sponsor or champion. The role of the champion is to be available whenever there is a logjam that needs management decision-making skills. For example, if there is a policy decision required that involves a change in the aftermarket service access to inventory on off hours, the champion would be the resource to help to arrange the right audience for this proposal and would coach the proposal itself to make sure it was appropriate for the business and market need.

Sponsor help does not stop there. Keep in mind that some of these team members may not be used to working in a team environment and may lack group decision-making, problem-solving, and/or meeting-efficiency skills. Guidance can include decision-making process coaching, system management advice, training time, additional resources, etc. It should go without saying that the champion must truly be a champion of the cause. If the top manager with the most passion for this improvement is not even in materials, then follow the passion. It has happened more than once that the CFO was the person most excited about this and was the right sponsor for inventory accuracy.

Problem-Solving Skills

Some teams will see success only after having some training and education in problem solving. In many organizations, as this process improvement was launched, the habits of the past did not prepare people with the proper problem-solving skills. The result was unprepared team members. Some of the simplest tools are the most effective. Examples of these simple tools include:

> **S**ome teams only do well after problem-solving training has been delivered to them successfully.

- **Brainstorming** — Brainstorming is the act of facilitating idea generation once a topic is defined as an objective. It is most effective when executed using agreed rules such as time frame, rules disallowing initial judgment of ideas during generation, and prioritization rules once the ideas are generated. As the process begins, describe the problem statement and ask for ideas that might affect the process outcome in a positive way. Do not judge the contributions until the team members have exhausted their imaginations. A good way to facilitate this is to go around the team in order and ask each person to contribute. Anyone who does not have a suggestion says "pass." Each time it is someone's turn as a team member, he or she can either contribute or pass. Members who have passed can contribute in the next turn if they are inspired by another team member's contribution. When everyone has passed in sequence, the evaluation phases can begin. These often can be best dealt with if they are grouped into categories. Once they are categorized, prioritize the categories by speed, ease, and impact. Those that can be done quickly and easily with decent impact would be the first ones to be assigned actions. Good process in this regard yields the best results from the time invested in this effort.

- **5-Why diagram** — One of the simplest problem-solving tools to use (after some practice) is the 5-why diagram. This tool is used to illustrate visually the possible causes of a given problem. The result is often to break a problem into workable pieces. A diagram and more detail will follow later in this book.

- **Pareto chart** — Pareto charts are useful tools for problem selection. They aid in the classification and interpretation of data as well as the prioritization of effects to the problem. Without understanding root cause of the variation in any problem statement, there is little chance of really eliminating the problem long term.

There are many more problem-solving tools that can be helpful for detecting and eliminating root causes. The simplest ones are those that stand the best chance of becoming habit. If these skills are not practiced and expected in every team effort, the cultural change will not be forthcoming.

Follow-Up Process

As the inventory accuracy project is established, there should be a clear understanding of the reporting schedule and structure expectations. Many high-performance initiatives use a management system that includes (at least) a weekly reporting cycle. In this review, the task team leader reports progress at the same time every week, without exception, to the management staff, sponsor, or steering committee. In a Class A ERP environment, this is referred to simply as the weekly performance review. The report should include:

- How much progress has been made in the past week?
- What are the accuracy measurements in each of the areas (warehouses, point of use, raw material storage area, raw material silos, etc.)?
- Which root cause activities are being discovered through cycle counting or control groups?
- What are the expected actions scheduled for the upcoming week?

This initial session with the team members should take approximately forty-five minutes to one hour and may be shorter as the team matures.

Days 2 and 3: Classroom Education

With the team empowered and workforce awareness heightened, the classroom education can now begin. On the second and third days, a comprehensive inventory accuracy course should be held with the team. This education should deal with a definition of inventory accuracy and why it is important to the organization. This initial education is extremely important to achieve employee understanding and, ultimately, acceptance of new inventory accuracy disciplines. It is often the introduction and first involvement for many of the employees to understand the need for procedural discipline. Unless your organization has an experienced specialist in inventory accuracy, an outside firm that specializes in this type of education often delivers the best results.

This education resource/consulting firm can create a common glossary of terms in the organization and ensure professional, accurate delivery of the material. The firm comes in without any bias toward existing procedures and, if the right organization is engaged, can be very helpful. In this regard, be cautious about hiring an outside organization that advertises to "do the work for you." When the organization with this approach has completed its assignment and leaves, the process will likely begin to decompose due to lack of ownership. Good consulting firms teach people to fish for themselves.

Organizations like the American Production and Inventory Control Society (APICS) can furnish materials that can be facilitated by internal resources or can also provide local skilled people to help facilitate. These local courses from APICS are usually done during the evening, as the instructors are normally not full

APICS can help by providing materials that are very appropriate for this endeavor.

time. Depending on the available resource, these people can be very helpful in giving an outside perspective on inventory accuracy. Facilitating materials can be especially effective on subsequent education. It is not always the best initial exposure in every situation.

Education does not end with this initial educational experience. Sharing the importance of inventory accuracy once with the employees is not enough of a catalyst to change the culture of a business. In most organizations, it is necessary to reinforce this new thinking several times before there is full support for the pending new practices and standards. This means education to understand the principles of enterprise resource planning (ERP), education on how data accuracy plays an integral part in the success of the organization, and instruction on how high-performance organizations improve their process controls for data accuracy. The intent is to develop the understanding throughout the workforce to ensure success (Figure 3-2).

Education is a fun and exciting part of the implementation of inventory accuracy. Many employees will be inspired by well-delivered sessions and will ask for more information. Additional sources of education such as ERP and supply chain video courseware are available on the market from organizations.

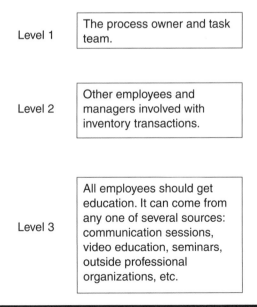

Figure 3-2.   Inventory accuracy education.

Getting the correct footing with the launch of this project will depend mostly on two initial efforts:

1. The communication and initial introduction to the workforce
2. The education quality delivered to the project team and key employees

Do not skimp or shortcut these steps in the process. Remember the payback and desires to accomplish this sustainable process improvement in the shortest time frame.

Education — the introduction of this process to the employees is key in making the correct first impressions. Do not skimp or shortcut this step in the process.

Now that the education has been started, the excitement has begun. The next phases will involve getting everyone further engaged and determining logical actions that must sequentially take place to successfully achieve 95 percent inventory record accuracy performance in the 120-day goal.

Summary

On day 1, management establishes the objective and picks a team for the successful completion of the objective. Day 1 initiates team empowerment. Days 2 and 3 bring the start of the classroom education. The implementation is well on its way toward changing the culture and habits of the organization.

4

Day 4: Discovering Transactions and Inventory Flow

Day 4

Step 1. Draw inventory flow diagram on facility blueprint.

Step 2. Indicate "staging" areas of inventory within the flow diagram.

Step 3. Document needed transactions for maintaining accuracy of these staged inventory areas.

Introduction

There is no better way to understand the process flow of a business than to draw it on a blueprint that depicts the facility layout. Many inventory movement transactions occur in most business processes. As data accuracy improvement is initiated, it is important to understand the number of transaction collection points, to understand the complexity of the transaction design, and to search for ways to simplify it.

In inventory record accuracy classes I have been involved with, attendees are asked how many different transaction types exist in their business systems to track and account for inventory movement. The answer is often twelve to fifteen different transaction types. Thinking about this concept, it might be valuable to assess how many transactions are really required to track inventory. The answers can range, but in reality the minimum is not controversial. There can be as few as two transactions in the simplest systems. While two probably does not make sense in most organizations, it does give one pause to think about the possibilities. In class, I jokingly refer to these as "inies" and "outies." Receipts and issues are all that really happens in affecting inventory balances. The fact that companies actually utilize a dozen different transactions just allows companies to do those two functions in ways to create data sorts later. These data sorts are helpful but can be overdone.

> **A** facility blueprint is an excellent tool to analyze and map the inventory flow process and understand the opportunities.

In Figure 4-1, location balance A is being reduced as inventory is moved to location B. At the same time, location B is being increased by the same amount. In this inventory movement, there is only one transaction affecting issues and one offsetting transaction affecting receipts. Most software systems will allow you to do several different transactions that affect inventory balances. These might include issuing quantities to scrap, receiving quantities from rework, issuing inventory for engineering tests, issuing units for sales samples, etc. For each different transaction type, several people are required to be versed and knowledgeable in the proper use of these transaction codes. Obviously, the fewer specific transaction types there are, the less to remember and the fewer mistakes.

Seem like too simple an idea? Today, software is flexible enough to accommodate almost any company's existing transaction processing system, good or bad. Remember that there are many organizations in existence that are less than world-class in performance. Software companies have to serve a wide range of customer needs, both good and bad. Do not

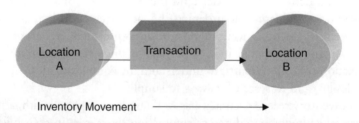

Figure 4-1. Inventory transaction design.

fall into this "multitransaction code" trap. It is advantageous to keep the process design simple. It is best to use no more than the minimum number of transaction codes. These generally would include scrap and rework as different transaction code designations and possibly a couple of codes defining the utilization of the part being issued. Remember also that one transaction code normally triggers both the issue and receipt for that particular movement. A part is moved from location A to location B. Location A is reduced with the issue and location B is increased with the receipt, all from one transaction code.

Software companies have to design and sell their products to all kinds of companies, both well and not well managed. It is wise to assess the options and features carefully before you use them all.

At the same time the organization is learning the existing transaction codes, it is helpful to develop a transaction matrix such as that shown in Table 4-1. This is simply a list of each transaction type with the resulting increases and decreases that occur by inventory location as material is transacted through the process.

Table 4-1 describes the effect of the actual transaction code used by the organization. Diagrams like this are helpful training tools for employees, especially employees who perform the mapped transactions. Building the flow documentation of various types creates a higher level of understanding necessary for proper problem solving and process improvement. By

Table 4-1. Transaction Matrix Showing Results of Each Transaction Type

Type/Code and Description	RAW	WIP123	WIP456	FG	AR
Production issue — move raw material from raw material stores to production	–	+			
Production receipt — finish production in area 123		–	+		
Production receipt — finish production in area 456			–	+	
Shipment — move inventory from FG to shipped status				–	+

RAW = raw material stores; WIP123 = work-in-process station #123; WIP456 = work-in-process station #456; G = finished goods inventory; AR = accounts receivable.

reviewing both a flow diagram and a transaction matrix, the team will get an appreciation for process design complexity and the benefits of simplification. Simplicity allows for easier training, fewer mistakes, and quicker results. Having to know just a few transaction types makes the accuracy of the transactions much more probable. Simple is good.

Simple is good when it comes to process design. That includes transaction design.

Inventory Flow Model and Process Maps

There are numerous advantages to developing process maps (see Figure 4-2 as an example). Here are just some of them:

1. Descriptive and informative for management
2. Easy to understand for employees

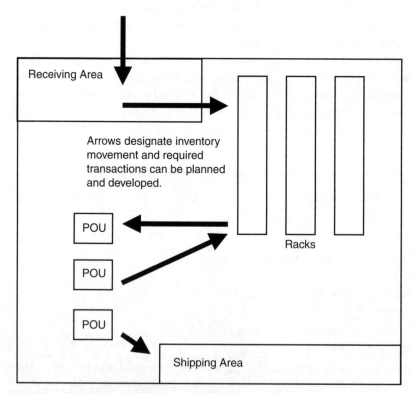

Figure 4-2. Transaction movement in the factory (POU = point of use).

3. Excellent training tool
4. Visual depiction simplifies many pages of written material
5. Describes categories of inventory (controlled versus process-driven work in process, etc.)
6. Becomes vehicle for discussing overall factory flow
7. Useful for period-to-period comparisons of progress

Bills of Material

It is also helpful at this early point in the implementation to document and understand the definition of commonly used terms in inventory accuracy initiatives. A glossary of terms will be built through the project. (For a good selection of terms you will probably run into, see the Glossary at the back of this book.) To start your glossary, the bill of material (BOM) is a good place to start. A BOM is a level-by-level structure of a product through the stages of conversion from raw materials through finished goods.

BOM design plays an important part in the transaction processing system. The levels in the BOM correspond with the structured relationship of all purchased materials and the manufacturing process. For each level in the BOM, transactions are required as material moves in and out of inventory (see Figure 4-3). The structure also displays the sourcing, either purchased or manufactured in-house. Any BOM level with no compo-

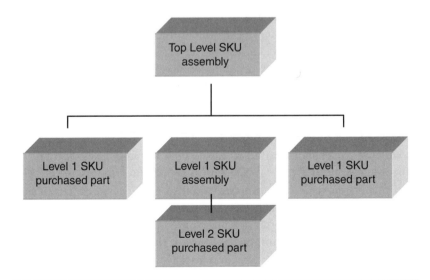

Figure 4-3. Sample BOM (SKU = stockkeeping unit).

nents called out is an outsourced or purchased component. At the same time, any BOM level with current components is a manufactured part, either an assembly or transformed component. A BOM level can show as few as one component although usually there are multiple components.

High-performance companies are just as serious about the elimination of levels in the BOM as they are about reducing inventory. Each level in the BOM requires transactions and adds to overall conversion cost. Even transactions that are system driven and automatically updated still require additional part numbers loaded and maintained in the system database. These transactions add unnecessary overhead to the processing system. The more levels, the more transactions; the more transactions, the more possibility of errors; the more errors, the more variation; the more variation, the more inventory required to offset the variation! It becomes very easy to see the impact of the BOM structure on system maintenance and overhead costs. As you can see, we are building on this concept of simplification for the sake of cost reduction and accuracy.

As shown in Figure 4-4, the BOM has five levels: level zero (0), level one (1), level two (2), level three (3), and level four (4). Each level represents an item that is either purchased or manufactured. The lowest level in the structure, level four, is purchased material. This is known because there are no components called out below level four items. When purchased raw materials or components are received at the manufacturer, a transaction is required to decrease on-order inventory and increase an on-hand balance. Level three items in this example could be fabricated parts, items that are made by altering or processing the raw materials in level four. When the level four raw material items are issued to the level three process, a transaction must occur to reduce the raw material on-hand balance. This reduces the on-hand balance of the level four items/material discussed previously. The level four materials are now positioned in the work in process (WIP) at level three. When the level three production is completed, a receipt transaction occurs to reduce WIP at level three and increase the on-hand balance of the level three item. This transaction processing continues through the entire BOM until the top-level (level zero) item is moved out of shipping in transit to the customer. Even then transactions occur to reduce on-hand inventory and add to accounts receivable. Because of this transaction requirement at each level, it is always a good idea to limit the number of levels in the BOM.

Some transactions can occur automatically, driven from either assumptions or events on the factory floor. Automatic deductions to inventory are

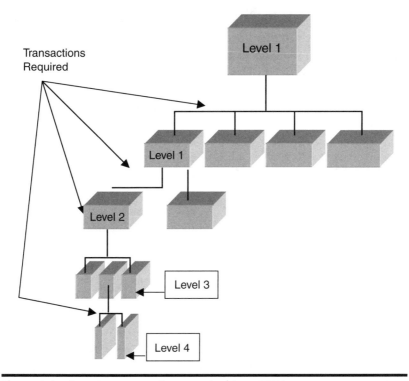

Figure 4-4. Inventory transactions required in a BOM.

BOM accuracy plays an important role in inventory accuracy, especially if automatic or back-flush transactions are utilized.

often referred to as "backflush" transactions. This will be discussed later in depth.

Accuracy of the BOM is especially important in these cases because planning systems utilize this information when calculating requirements for raw material and component inventory quantities. Accuracy in part number structure, quantity required, and unit of measure is a requirements for BOM accuracy.

An Example of What Can Be Accomplished

In the early 1990s, a medium-sized capital goods manufacturer in New York generated a specific focus to save monies in the area of BOM-level reduction. A study evidenced that there were, on average, thirteen levels in its BOM structure from raw material to completed machine. Maybe more importantly, it was also discovered through study and learning that having those thirteen levels in the BOM structure added significant system overhead in transactions and complexity to the design structure. Interestingly, no one had questioned this over the years.

After the Class A ERP (enterprise resource planning) team finished its study, the decision was made and supported by top management to limit the number of BOM levels to four with all new product introductions. That meant that no new products, regardless of complexity, could be introduced with over four levels in the BOM structure. In this environment, the engineering BOM was also the manufacturing BOM. This is common practice in high-performance organizations today.

> In high-performance organizations, it is common practice that the engineering BOM is also the manufacturing BOM.

There was initial resistance to this change, especially from engineering, but as the idea took shape on new products and the engineers began to apply the concept, the result was much simpler design structures. This change positively affected inventory levels required, lead time, and costs. Looking back on it, it was an idea that should have been implemented years before. The only thing that stopped it was that nobody had ever questioned the need for thirteen levels, nor why it had initially been designed as a common practice. It was one of those infamous "it's always been done" things.

In another interesting example of BOM application, I was asked by a urethane manufacturing client in Massachusetts to help interview candidates for a newly created master scheduling position. One individual was a seemingly qualified candidate from a large defense contract manufacturer. (This contractor manufactures large pieces of equipment for the U.S. Army. I will not say what, because it will give the name away and I do not want to embarrass anyone!)

During the discussion, the candidate, when asked about his experience in using BOM design for competitive advantage, bragged that his organization had over one hundred BOM levels in many of its designs! He was proud of his ability to work in such a complex environment. I thought I had seen and heard everything concerning bad practice with BOM design, but was proven wrong that day. I had never known any organization to stray that far from logic. As you can imagine, he did not get the position. It may also help explain the high costs of military equipment. If you have first-hand knowledge of who this is and have any influence there, please exercise it for us taxpayers!

Table 4-2.   Typical Goals Established by Top-Performing Manufacturing Companies

Product	Maximum Levels in BOM
Molded/extruded plastic parts	3 (raw mat, batch, FG)
Plastic assemblies	3 (raw mat, batch, FG)
Baked goods	3 (raw mat, batch, FG)
Sheet metal fabricating	4 (raw mat, fabricate, weld, FG/assy)
Capital equipment	4 (raw mat, fabricate, weld/subassy, FG/assy)
Electronic	3 (raw, sub assy, FG/assy)

Raw mat = raw material; batch = blended level of raw material; fabricate = fabricated part from raw material; FG = finished goods level, typically an assembly in these examples; assy = assembly including subassemblies.

Recommended/optimum levels in a BOM. Note that in some businesses, the processes would have to be simplified to allow for these BOM structures.

BOM levels are of concern in high-performance companies. The less levels, the fewer transactions required.

Not only does accuracy in the BOM become important in an ERP environment, so does the BOM structure. In many high-performance organizations, there are no more than four levels in the BOM. Table 4-2 shows some typical goals established by top-performing manufacturing companies.

Unit of Measure

The component-to-parent relationship in a BOM is stated in both part numbers (or item numbers) and quantities required. To have complete understanding of the quantity required, a unit of measure is needed. Units of measure can be stated in inches, linear feet, square feet, cubic feet, pounds, tons, cases, each, and numerous other possibilities. A common problem for organizations is the use of multiple units of measures in the same BOM, such as feet and inches. This can be problematic at best and disastrous at worst.

An example of potential problems caused by multiple units of measure happened at the same capital equipment manufacturing company in upstate New York referenced earlier. In this example, half-inch wall, square tubes were purchased in ten-foot lengths for spacers. The spacer simply changed the width of the finished product depending on the customer

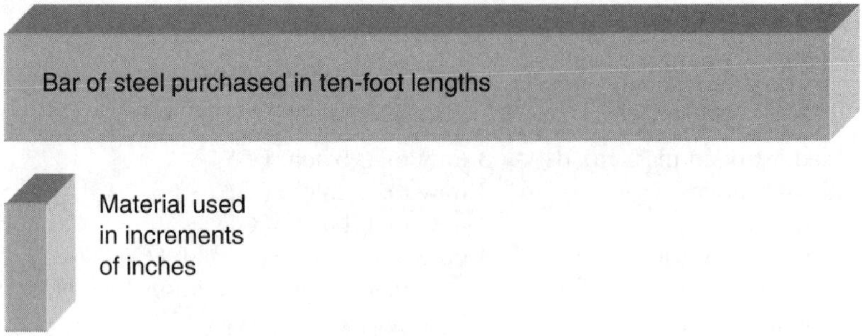

Bar of steel purchased in ten-foot lengths

Material used
in increments
of inches

Figure 4-5. Confusion can happen from materials with more than one unit of measure.

application. It was a key in the flexibility of design and eliminated the need for more complex redesign requirements. These spacers were typically a few inches in length, with two required on each machine, one on the left-hand side and one on the right-hand side of the machine body.

The raw material was purchased in tube lengths from a local steel supplier (Figure 4-5). The supplier sold the required tubes in ten-foot lengths and considered and invoiced each length as one piece (ten feet long). The unit of measure on the computer-based purchasing system at the machine manufacturer for these tubes was pieces (each); however, the unit of measure in the BOM developed by engineering was in inches. Are you getting the picture? Engineering specified a requirement in the drawing for the required inches of tubing on each side of the weldment.

To complicate matters further, at the same time of this story, the tubing lengths were moved to a new planner/buyer who had the responsibility to plan and order the material in question from the steel supplier. Requirements from the material requirements planning (MRP) system calculated, netted out, and generated quantity schedules for the unit of measure called out in the BOM. As stated, the BOM was in inches of tubing, as engineering had determined the need in each design. The buyer/planner would react to the MRP signal and send a purchase order release to the supplier based on the calculated requirement. (If fifty inches were required for the released batch of requirements, the planner would get a signal to order fifty.) Note that in the past, a conversion was done by the planner who knew about this conversion issue. The conversion was necessary because the part number in the item master, accurately, showed the tube as a ten-foot piece.

Since there were "several" inches required per day for the master production schedule, the quantity per day ordered from the supplier by this new planner/buyer was also "several." The resulting "several" was of the ten-foot pieces; however, no conversion was done! It was not until the warehouse manager inquired as to why these tubes were bought in such large quantities that the problem was identified. By then, the outside pole-barn used to store tubing was full. The problem was solved easily by converting the purchasing unit of measure to inches through agreements with the supplier. The minimum buy quantity became ten-feet worth of inches or 1200 inches. With the two records now in sync, MRP did not signal the planner to order additional 1200-inch minimum buys until the reorder point was met. While this seems like a rare problem, it is not. It happens all the time with smaller parts. The smaller parts just do not get the same publicity.

Routings

A routing record is a record that houses the sequence of operations with work center locations (machine or work cells) and operational times (referred to as standards) established. Like a road map, it describes how raw material and/or components travel through the manufacturing process for transformation into saleable items through each level in the BOM. All the stopping points are identified.

Routings not only describe process sequence, but they also can be used to track material in process. WIP inventory balances are perpetual records of inventory flow through the manufacturing or conversion process maintained in the business system. The routing record is the map that describes the planned flow.

In some business systems today, the routing record is used directly in conjunction with the BOM record. These hybrid records are often referred to as bills of resource (BORs). They document all of the conversion characteristics: sequence of process, sequence of material usage, specific components, and some cost factors.

Even with all of this discussion on the topic of routing records, it must be noted that in most high-performance companies today, routings have taken a reduced role. Rather than the basis for locating specific jobs in the shop as in the days of *expediting,* today routings have been simplified. The improvement reflects management awareness of cost and process variation opportunities. The revised routing record reflects the movement to work cells and process flow. These simplified routings now combine many operations done in a work cell, documenting the summary steps. This has simplified the inventory tracking system and improved inventory record accuracy as well.

Rather than a routing described as:

Sequence	Operation	Work Center
Operation 010	Saw to length	7230
Operation 020	Grind	3410
Operation 030	Mill surface	5600
Operation 040	Delivery to weld area	6300

the routing might instead simply read:

Sequence	Operation	Work Cell
Operation 010	Complete part	2200

In some organizations, either labor transactions (transactions that indicate to the computer system that an operation within the routing has been completed) or shop-floor inventory transactions updating the production status will trigger increases and decreases to inventory balances. Often this is done through the use of automatic transactions sometimes referred to as *backflushing*.

Backflushing

Backflushing is a method to relieve inventory of components and materials used in the manufacturing or conversion process automatically. As product moves through the manufacturing process, the movement can trigger consumption of lower level materials, based on the BOM. The quantity of product is valued by the quantity per unit of all components/ ingredients within the associated BOM. At the same time, these quantities are relieved from the on-hand inventories for each item. The need to manually issue material to a factory order or schedule is thereby eliminated. Backflushing can result in significant reductions in paperwork and manual transactions.

While backflushing can reduce transaction collection and entry costs, its use can also result in inaccurate inventory records. The difficulties encountered with backflushing usually fall into two categories: incorrect BOM records and reporting accuracy. Errors in reporting the quantity of items completed in production as well as existing BOM errors are processed into the inventory system automatically using backflushing. Unreported material substitution or inaccurate or missing scrap transactions also translate into inaccurate

While backflushing may reduce transaction collection costs, its use can also contribute to inventory inaccuracies.

inventory records. Timing of these additional transactions (such as the scrap and substitutions) must be real time to ensure that inventory records and actual inventory balances agree. In many organizations that use backflush transactions, this discipline does not exist.

To discuss an example, if there is a point-of-use (POU) storage area adjacent to an assembly area in a manufacturing process where components are stored, somehow the issue and receipt transactions must occur to affect the inventory balance of the component. One way to have that happen is to show issues from the source to the POU storage location.

As shown in Figure 4-6, if a supplier delivers the component directly to the assembly area, the invoice from the supplier might trigger a receipt transaction to the POU1 location. If there is an assembly requiring this component, an issue transaction from POU1 to the assembly WIP part number must happen. This transaction can be done manually by typing the transaction code and quantity into the system, thus relieving the balance. When backflushing is utilized, the direct labor employee clocking on or off the WIP-level shop order triggers both the issue transaction from storage and the receipt transaction to WIP. In repetitive environments, where work orders are not used, the labor transaction against a scheduled quantity can trigger the same sequence of events.

Figure 4-6 reflects a "postproduction backflush." There are also other transactions that trigger backflushing. A backflush can be triggered as material is delivered to the worksite (Figure 4-7), and backflushing can also occur as the work begins.

If there is inaccuracy in either the BOM or the quantity reported on the labor transaction, the resulting balance will be incorrect. At that point, the efficiency of the transaction is lost in the cost of the inaccuracy. These costs can include inventory buffer levels to cover the variation, expedite costs, priority freight, continuing need for a periodic physical inventory, and customer service.

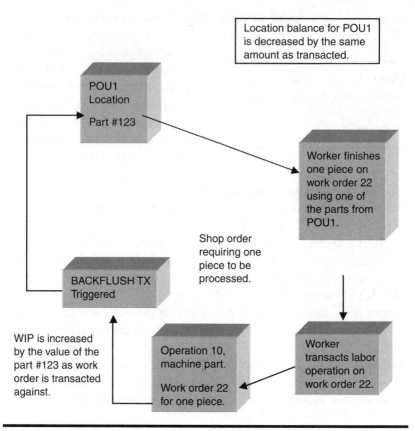

Figure 4-6.   Backflushing.

Another frequently experienced problem with backflushing is the length of time that transpires between material moving into the manufacturing process and the backflush transaction timing. When backflushing is used to relieve inventory, the location balance will show an inaccurate amount in stock until the triggering transaction is executed. If it takes, for example, three hours from the time the job is kitted and moved into the assembly area until the time a triggering transaction is done, the inventory balance for the kitted components will show an inflated quantity during the three hours. If a cycle count was done during the three-hour

Be wary of backflushing as there can be limitations and problems associated with its use. Use backflushing only when it is low risk to inventory accuracy.

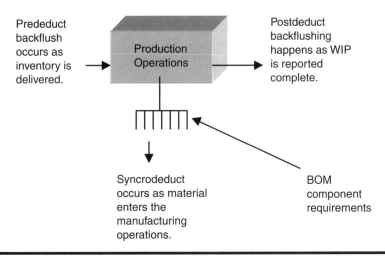

Figure 4-7. Timing of backflushing.

time period, reconciliation would have to occur to verify accuracy in the inventory record.

As previously mentioned, there are some assumptions made when backflushing is utilized to adjust inventory balances or transact inventory movement:

1. All scrap is reported accurately and in a timely manner.
2. All substitutions are documented and reported.
3. BOMs are 100 percent accurate
4. Predefined locations are actually used.
5. No significant delay between usage and actual backflush triggering transaction.

If scrap or substitutions are not reported accurately and in a timely manner, backflushing will lead to inaccuracies in balances. If the BOM has the wrong part number called out in its component list or the quantity required on the BOM is inaccurate, the backflushing transaction will result in continually inaccurate inventory records. The need for periodic physical inventories can never be eliminated when these variations occur.

Now that I have bad-mouthed backflushing thoroughly, it needs to be said that backflushing is used somewhere in almost every manufacturing business. There are specific places that it makes a lot of sense and should be implemented. Within WIP, in a lean operation, it almost always makes sense, as fast-moving inventory cannot be counted and transaction points happen so fast from one operation to the next that it would be foolish to do any other type of transaction short of not doing one at all. In many such operations, feeder lines are moving directly into an assembly operation in one piece or otherwise small mixed model quantities. No one would want to do all the necessary transactions for the feeder line parts. For this reason, WIP is often a reasonable application for backflushing.

Transaction Process Flow for Inventory Accuracy

Variability in the manufacturing process is a given in every company. The only differentiator is how much variation. While this may not seem like an ideal thought or optimistic outlook, variation exists and we need to acknowledge it. Yield rate is a measurement used to understand some of this variability. Companies that measure first-time quality often use a yield rate factored into their BOM structure to represent the quantity expected to result in production. These yield rates are seldom accurately predictable from one production run to the next. After all, if the process is repeatable, usually this variation level can be minimized. These organizations also often still use backflushing to issue inventory to customer or production orders. These yield rates can play havoc with inventory balances.

If inventory balances are to be kept accurate, in these cases, it is often helpful to segregate controlled stores inventory from WIP or POU inventory. The recommended way to ensure that there will be accurate inventory balances for each category of inventory is to segregate the raw and finished goods inventory from the WIP inventory. Think of it as painting a line on the floor around WIP and therefore segregating both raw material and finished goods. Once this line of demarcation is both painted and communicated, a manual (nonbackflush) transaction should be done every time a part or group of parts crosses the line. Figure 4-8 shows the transaction requirements.

As shown in the figure, a transaction most likely would be performed by the material handler or dispatcher. To maintain accuracy, this transaction is done at the same time the material actually moves. By having this transaction control point at entry and exit from WIP, the accuracy of both raw and finished goods is assured (once disciplines are in place). In effect, variability from the manufacturing process is isolated within WIP using this transaction process design. This is the method most organizations with high accuracy use to keep controls tight on manufacturing inventories.

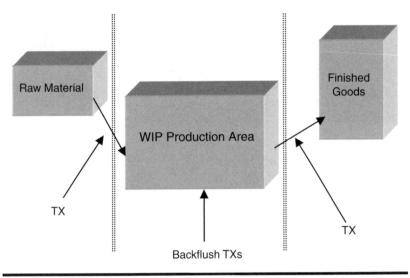

Figure 4-8. Building artificial walls around WIP (TX = inventory transaction).

Finished goods inventory is usually the most accurate area in a factory regardless of the discipline focus. The desire is always high and the finance people are usually watching closely. This makes the point that it is not that difficult. By isolating the raw materials and components, it should start to be easier there, too.

Work-in-Process Storage

In many high-performance organizations, inventory is stored on the assembly line. In more contemporary environments, the replenishment is done by suppliers. This storage area is still a controlled area and should be aligned with the perpetual record in the business system. The barrier line of control still needs to be drawn around the storage areas, but in this case the line just goes out into the production areas. This is not to be confused with WIP. Sometimes it means drawing a line around locations in the shop. Figure 4-9 gives an idea of what this might look like.

The WIP storage areas in the diagram are simply extensions of the raw material warehouse. The rules are the same as is the transaction design. Backflushing may be used in some of these applications, but should be avoided where high probability of process variation exists.

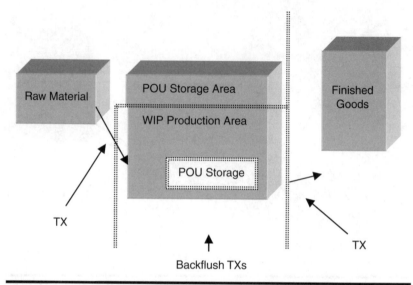

Figure 4-9. Building artificial walls around WIP when POU storage is used (TX = inventory transaction).

The Lines on the Floor

When the warehouse perimeter lines are painted on the floor to designate the proper placement and quantity of inventory, they should be treated with the same discipline as if there were a locked fence in place. When done with honest effort, they actually can be more effective than the fence alone. This type of focus requires management backing and discipline to be administered consistently through all shifts and with all employees. No one should be "privileged" and allowed to shortcut the system, especially management.

At one appliance manufacturer in Tennessee, the painted lines represent the demarcation just as if a stockade were in place. The company goes one refreshing step farther. It differentiates the area even more inside the painted lines with requirements of dress. To set the stage for discipline, authorization is a prerequisite for entering the storeroom. Because of this rule, when some-

> In the beginning, limiting access to stores may seem counter to customer service instincts, but over time you will find that customer service actually improves.

one is physically in the controlled storage area (inside the painted lines), he or she has to show authorization. Part of the proof of authorization is demonstrated by the wearing of a bright yellow vest with reflective tape. This is issued as a person enters. While safety is also probably helped by these bright vests in high-traffic storage areas, the real reason is to create a psychological barrier around this important storage area. When people enter the storage area wearing this vest, they are well aware of different behavior requirements. Management enforces this rule enthusiastically, and because of this support, it has been very effective. If you are in the area without a vest, you are asked to leave. It works.

In yet another example, yellow hard hats were required of anyone inside the stores area. This organization was equally effective. In both cases, management was aware of the importance of this discipline. These two examples represent innovative thinking and a commitment to accuracy through proper disciplines.

Is Backflushing a Good Idea?

In manufacturing operations within the WIP area, where the process is both repetitive and more predictable, backflushing may offer a reasonable solution for ease of transaction processing. The advantage of backflushing is that it reduces labor involved in executing the transactions. In actuality, there are few organizations that do not use some form of backflushing successfully and effectively somewhere in their operation. The trick is to limit backflushing to areas where control is either very disciplined, such as in a small, very well-managed, controlled stores area with little yield variation, or where the risks are not as high, such as between operations in WIP.

> The trick is to limit backflushing to areas where control is either very disciplined, such as in a small, very well-managed, controlled stores area with little yield variation, or where the risks are not as high, such as between operations in WIP.

Scrap and yield transactions, again, play a big part in the decision as to where these automatic transactions are appropriate. I go with the rule that nothing is ever free. If you think backflushing is a free transaction, think again. What you save in transaction labor you may pay later in expediting costs.

Summary

Whichever method an organization chooses to transact activity and balance updates, discipline is a requirement. Part of discipline support comes from good documentation. The inventory transaction flow should be diagrammed and agreed to by the employees involved. This documentation becomes the model to measure, to audit against, and for training personnel. There will be more about documentation later. At this point in the implementation, the emphasis should still be on what good process design would look like.

5

Day 5–45:
Control Groups and
Root Cause Analysis

Day 5 through 45

Step 1. Establish the control group.

Step 2. Reconcile balances daily — understand the reason for inaccuracy.

Step 3. Implement root cause analysis.

Step 4. Eliminate barriers to data accuracy and report performance weekly.

Step 5. Achieve control group accuracy of 100 percent for ten working days.

Step 6. Start new control group.

Step 7. Implement standard cycle counting.

Companies frequently reconcile inventory through physical inventory counts or periodic cycle counts. Unfortunately, too many of these organizations really are engaged in just "fixing bad balances." Like perpetual cleansing, the counts are designed simply to clean up ongoing errors that happen unacknowledged. This is not the case in high-performance operations.

A distribution warehouse in Michigan reported an accuracy of 95 percent and does a full warehouse count every month through its cycle count process. That means that its cycle count program randomly selects location balances every day to count. Enough counts are made to ensure that the entire warehouse is counted by the time four weeks have passed.

Cycle counting done correctly is not counting to fix bad balances. It is about checking to see if process control is being maintained as planned.

If you assume that the cycle counts are relatively accurate and that the inaccuracies are fixed as found within the four-week cycle, then with a posted accuracy of 95 percent, one can assume that at least a 5 percent variation factor is added each and every month. If cycle counts were stopped, the accuracy would fall logically to 90 percent in two months and 85 percent in three. When you look at it this way, it is much less satisfying to brag about a 95 percent performance level.

Normally, A items, those inventoried items highest in value, are cycle counted fully every quarter at the most. In the Michigan example, if the company had control of its process variation, it could take the resources used for cycle counting and defer them to other higher value-added activities.

One of the easiest ways to uncover error causes in balance inaccuracies is to implement control groups. They are effective in determining the sources of the process variation.

Understanding and eliminating the reasons for inventory inaccuracy is a productive use of resource and eventually results in much less expense to maintain accuracy. One of the easiest ways to uncover the barriers to consistent accuracy of inventory records (determining root cause) is to implement *control groups* in preparation for cycle counting.

Control Groups

An inventory accuracy control group is a select group of fast-moving parts or component materials that are counted repeatedly to determine, reconcile, and eliminate the causes of inventory record inaccuracy. It is important to select items/materials for the control group that have high activity. This assures exposure to error-causing events and/or inaccurate process inputs. This control group should also be representative of the total population of parts/materials.

Step 1: Determine Control Group

To start an effective control group, choose thirty to fifty item number locations with high activity. These materials should also be a reasonable representation or sampling of the kinds of materials or parts used in the process. It also makes sense to pick stockkeeping units (SKUs) from various areas rather than all from the same area and they should be higher volume parts to make sure there is activity during the control group period.

The ultimate objective of this control group methodology is to ensure a controlled process and account accurately for inventory movement so that variation causes can be determined. Individual item location balances (rather then the total item balance of all locations) can be part of the thirty to fifty balances required for this step.

If there is a question as to how many locations should be counted, the answer is simple. There is a mandatory requirement to reconcile the variation to root cause each day for inaccurate balances found. If there is too much variation to keep up with and you find yourself not being able to reconcile fully each day, you have too many location balances being counted. On the other hand, if you do not find enough location balance variation with the number of locations being counted, you may want to add more locations. This will begin to make more sense as the full control group methodology is explained.

On the morning of the first day, count all of the items or locations in the control group. Next, match the count quantity to the data record file (on the computer) and reconcile any differences. At this point, the objective is to be assured that the computer record is accurate as the control group process is started. It is important to have an accurate starting point for the implementation of the control group. If any of the balances do not correspond with the perpetual computer record, count them again to ensure accuracy in the count. If this is not followed, you will end up on the proverbial "wild goose chase." Once you have the accurate balances documented, you are prepared for the next step.

Step 2: Repeat Process to Discover Inaccuracy

On the second day, you are going to repeat the exact same process. You will count the same control group of item location balances and match the quantity counted with the computer inventory records just as you did on the first day. The purpose of this second count is to see if the process variation has shown its ugly head. Usually, if there is variation occurring regularly and you have chosen high-activity locations for the exercise, finding variation will not be difficult. Say, as an example, that four location balances in the control group counted have become inaccurate since the previous day's count. Some very important information is known at this point, and it is at this point that the value of this process becomes apparent. In this case and all others you know:

1. These four inventory balances had activity. If you picked the correct balances for this test, you should be confident that there was activity in each of these locations during the test.
2. Transactions were not aligned with physical movement of inventory. The simple fact that four of the balances in the example were out of line is an indicator that transactions, for some reason, were not in synchronization.
3. The most important piece of information, however, is the simplest. The error happened in the last twenty-four hours. Too many times, it is impossible to know when the error occurred, which makes it very difficult to diagnose.

It is critically important to find and document the root cause of any errors from the control group within twenty-four hours of the detection. Without this timely action, it is sometimes impossible to find out what process control collapsed or was missing to cause the inaccuracy. This is precisely the problem with a periodic physical inventory count. Many transactions for the item may need to be reviewed just to attempt to understand the root cause of the error. The objective of a control group is to find the variation or problem in the transaction processing system and fix it. Use the people performing inventory transactions in the control group activity to eliminate the accuracy errors. This will ensure user understanding of any changes to the process, understanding of the process controls, and will ultimately result in process predictability. It means getting process controls in place for inventory record accuracy.

> **U**se the people performing the transactions in the control group inventory to work the process changes. They are the closest to the problems.

It should be noted here that the recommended thirty to fifty locations is a rule of thumb. As causes are determined, the number of items in the control group should be adjusted to the "right" amount of material or items for the group. As suggested earlier, the "right" amount could be defined as enough locations counted daily to find problems, but not so many as to be unable to reconcile the problems daily. Between thirty and fifty item locations is usually the right number of high-activity locations to check daily, but is not exact as each situation is different. You will have to experiment a bit in the beginning to determine the correct amount. Errors are gems and should be cherished in this process.

Each day the objective is to determine and document the root cause for each inaccuracy in the control group count. It is important to find the source or root cause of the problem creating the inaccuracy so that action can be taken to eliminate these barriers to high-performance inventory record accuracy. Examples could include:

1. Parts have been moved without the proper corresponding inventory transaction.
2. Parts were not received correctly from a supplier.
3. The supplier sent in a different count than was documented on the packing slip and no verification count was made.
4. Lack of proper training resulted in inaccurate picking by a new employee.
5. Scrap was made but not accounted for properly with a corresponding transaction.
6. etc.

Once the reasons for errors are understood, a measurement document should be created to depict and communicate the facts surrounding inaccuracy of inventory records. A Pareto chart (see Figure 5-1 for an example) works well to display errors and frequency of occurrence visually. Pareto analysis allows the emphasis to be targeted at the biggest offenders of accuracy.

(Sample) Reason Definitions:
1. Parts moved without the corresponding transaction
2. Inaccurate picking from warehouse
3. Parts not received correctly from a supplier
4. Scrap not accounted for in production
5. Production personnel sending parts back into the warehouse with inaccurate transactions

Reasons will vary from company to company, plant to plant, department to department. Your reason codes may be different than those in the

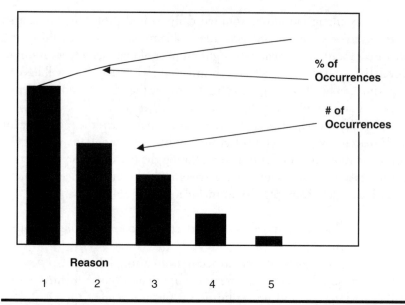

Figure 5-1.   Pareto of causes as discovered in control group A. Each bar represents the volume of occurrences of a specific root cause. By charting them this way, emphasis can be centered on the worse offenders.

sample model. It is an extremely useful exercise to document the errors causing variation in the process accurately.

Step 3: Find Root Cause

Once facts are gathered concerning the reasons for record inaccuracy, find the root cause for the reason. Often what warehouse or inventory managers find at this stage is that people do not understand the procedures, process disciplines are not being enforced, suppliers are not holding quantity to the same level of accuracy that they do dimensional tolerances, or there are inaccuracies in the bill of material records caused by a lack of proper standards. All of these can be dealt with easily. The prerequisite is acknowledgment of this variation.

The best way to be assured of root cause is to make sure it is actionable. Although not completely foolproof even then, it is a good indicator.

There is no real fail-safe or mistake-proof method to determine root cause. Root cause can be deceptive. The best way to be sure you have arrived at root cause is to determine what action can be driven as a result of knowing the data. Many times, problem solvers will believe they have achieved root cause only to find out that there are more underlying causes beneath the data.

5-Why Diagramming

One approach that helps to ensure success in finding real root cause is to apply the proven "5-why" method, also sometimes called "5-why diagramming." This detailed problem-solving methodology is also one of the most simple to use. When reasons for inaccuracy are determined initially, ask why five times or until there is clear requirement for corrective action. For each reason, a "reason tree" begins to develop. These reason trees are the basis for understanding real root cause. This exercise can take a lot of wall space or flip chart pages if done correctly. A 5-why diagram can be very easy to use and is very effective in peeling back layers of a given problem or opportunity.

When using a 5-why diagram, the group would start by defining the problem statement (see Figure 5-2). For example, an error has been uncovered where the first level of why for inaccuracy is "materials moved without the proper corresponding transactions." This is obviously not the root cause yet. In this first why, not much beyond the problem statement has been determined.

The second why in the 5-why diagram might be:

1. There is not a clearly defined procedure established and published for the correct actions surrounding transactions.
2. Some transactions are not covered by the original intent of the system design.
3. People have been replaced over the years and training has not been maintained properly.

Even in this example there may be another "why" required to uncover the real cause. Asking why has to be done until it becomes obvious what plan of action needs to be initiated. Let's pursue the first "why," as stated: "There is not a clearly defined procedure established and published for the correct actions surrounding transactions." "Why" needs to be asked again. The second level of why might yield the reasons:

1. Management has not required documentation.
2. There is no central repository for procedural documentation.

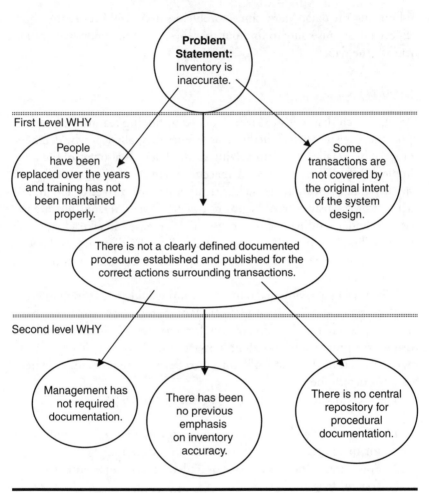

Figure 5-2. Sample 5-why diagram.

   3. There has been no previous emphasis on inventory accuracy prior
      to this focus.

The list could go on. Either each of these could be determined as
actionable or another level of "why" could be documented. The process
goes on until there is a clear path of action that everyone agrees is a
reasonable plan for improvement. There are other tools that can be used
in this step, but the 5-why diagram is a very useful one.

Step 4: Eliminate the Reason

Knowing the reason for inaccuracy leads to the next logical and necessary step — eliminating the reason for inaccuracy. Corrective actions must result from the learning if the control group is to be effective. Often these actions are in the form of improved documentation of procedures, more frequent audits of procedures being followed, and better training in proper procedures and company policies. Sustainable process requires a robust management system. In high-performance organizations, process owners report performance at some form of management system event. One of the best formats is a formal weekly performance review process (where management observes progress reports in a predictable meeting held the same time each week and it is regarded as an important part of how the business is managed). The actions resulting from the root cause analysis should be reported at this meeting. More on the weekly performance review will follow (see Chapter 11).

Step 5: Achieve Accuracy

The expected result of root cause analysis and resulting corrective actions will be the achievement of 100 percent accuracy in the original control group. Step five is to achieve control group accuracy for ten consecutive error-free workdays. This accomplishment will be a significant progress gate. Ten error-free days is an indication that the process is in control — for the control group! Since the control group is a representation of the total population of inventory balances, it is a reasonable assumption that the errors that were uncovered and eliminated in the control group were also being committed throughout the facility.

It is important to understand the realities — sometimes there will be a heightened awareness of the original control group after a few days of counting the same parts over and over. Heightened awareness can lead to artificial process control that will not be sustainable over time nor necessarily applied consistently over the entire base of parts or inventory.

Step 6: Verify Process Control

Having the original control group at 100 percent accuracy is great indeed! It is good, however, to verify that the newly installed process control is also in control outside the original control group. Verify your process control success by sample testing with a second control group. The same process from the original control group (control group A) is repeated. The only difference is the list of materials or parts. This time, companies often choose a larger quantity of items to count since the errors should be infrequent or eliminated completely. The same rules apply — if the errors are in line with the ability to keep up with daily reconciliation to root cause, the correct number of counts is being made. Remember, the idea is to find errors if they exist.

Step 7: Cycle Counting

After the second control group verifies process control, a standard/traditional cycle counting program is appropriate. In a standard cycle counting process, a planned schedule ensures that all parts are counted adequately annually. One popular method has the count frequency of each part dependent on value and/or volume usage of each individual material or part (for a full explanation of cycle counting methods, see Chapter 9).

Problem-Solving Tools

During the control group process, it becomes clear how important problem-solving skills are. It is important to understand both root cause and how to use this information to drive appropriate corrective actions. In many organizations, the team responsible for data accuracy is made up of warehouse pickers and cycle counters. They do not always have the required training in problem-solving tools. Too many organizations do not regularly supply this training except for management-level people. If this is the case in your organization, education and training must be a part of the data accuracy process implementation.

The tools do not have to be sophisticated or complicated. The simplest tools, in fact, are typically the best. Examples of simple problem-solving tools include fishbone analysis, brainstorming, 5-why diagramming (covered earlier), and Pareto analysis.

Fishbone Method

The fishbone method is an easily understood and executed, yet powerful, problem-solving tool. Using the fishbone to understand root cause can be an easily administered methodology. People who have little experience with problem-solving tools are normally quick to respond to this method.

The fishbone method of root cause analysis is used to remind the team members that there are numerous sources of process variation. It is normal for team members to have preconceived ideas about these causes, but by opening up the discussion and searching for all the possible sources, many times learning happens and the team members can find that their assumptions are not as solid as they thought. Even when opinions do not necessarily change, the opportunity to use this tool still offers the chance of finding additional sources of variation worth pursuing.

The rules are simple:

1. Develop a problem statement for the exercise.
2. Draw the fishbone diagram on a white board or flip chart as the process begins.
3. Label the legs of the fishbone with the 4 Ms and environment (see Figure 5-3).
4. Start with one leg (manpower, for example). Have each team member, one at a time, brainstorm possibilities for the cause of the problem within the manpower source. After this leg seems to have been exhausted, continue through the others (methods, machinery, etc.) until all are completed with the team's input.
5. Prioritize the root cause possibilities using criteria of:
   - Likelihood of impact to problem statement
   - Ease of confirmation
   - Data availability

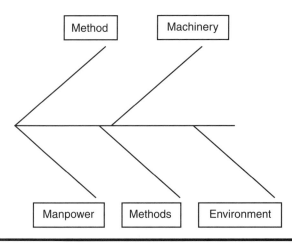

Figure 5-3. Fishbone diagram.

6. Assign team members to collect data and report back to the group on results.
7. Once the data have been collected, actions are to follow.
8. Results should be posted visibly to involve other employees in the process. When others are made aware of problem-solving activities, valuable input that is otherwise unsolicited often will be forthcoming.

Brainstorming

Brainstorming has been around for a long time and is probably the tool used most often and also the tool *misused* most often. Good brainstorming starts with the rules well understood and a facilitator ready to enforce those rules. The rules generally are:

1. No ideas are judged until the possibilities are exhausted. This means that as ideas are offered, no comments like "that idea has little merit" (or other less polite comments) are allowed even though they may seem appropriate. Experience proves that some of the craziest ideas in sessions like these either end up not being so crazy or may spur additional ideas that may not have been thought of. Eliminating ideas at this point or intimidating team members not to offer them is a mistake and degrades the process.
2. Have each team member, in order of seating sequence, offer an idea. If any team member has exhausted all of his or her ideas at that point, he or she can pass but must say "pass" each time his or her turn comes up. This forces each team member to be part of the process and eliminates the possibility of all ideas coming from one bulldozing team member. By allowing multiple passes, if a team member who has previously passed has an idea generated from one offered by another team member, he or she will still have the opportunity (almost obligation) to submit it.
3. When everyone has passed twice, the consolidation and prioritization begin. Prioritization generally starts with pulling similar ideas together into categories or topics. By consolidating the ideas, resulting assignments become much more realistic and organized. Once the categories are settled, a prioritization process begins.
4. Prioritization is normally based on two criteria:
   - Impact
   - Ease of implementation or investigation

5. Action assignments follow.
6. As with other problem-solving methods, results should be posted visibly to involve other employees in the process.

Pareto

Pareto analysis was discussed briefly earlier in this chapter. It is also a very helpful, yet simple, tool for aligning resource to the most frequent cause or variation. The real added value that the Pareto chart gives is its factual nature and automatic prioritization of root causes. It does this through the collection and display of data in order of occurrence. As we saw in Figure 5-1, there is a higher occurrence in the left-most bar. When getting data collection directly for a control group process, the Pareto becomes especially valuable. It allows easy emphasis on the worst reasons for inventory inaccuracy and, accordingly, the most effective actions to be assigned.

The Pareto can be used in conjunction with the other tools described. For example, information gathered from brainstorming will lead to data gathering around certain categories of variation. These data can then be applied to a Pareto chart. The same would be true for fishbone analysis.

Many high-performance organizations hold educational sessions in the use of problem-solving tools prior to establishing process improvement teams. This can make the teams much more effective and can lead to faster improvement. Teams that conquer the use of these tools are typically the teams that go on to solve other more challenging problems, eventually allowing achievement of Class A ERP (enterprise resource planning) performance levels not only in areas of data accuracy but also other important process control areas. By using this approach specifically in inventory accuracy and with a control group methodology, the best results can be expected. Employees will be more engaged and will own the results more readily.

Steps for Problem Solving
1. Management sponsors a project.
2. A team is picked.
3. Team leader is picked.
4. The team participates in a refresher problem-solving course.
5. Meeting schedule is determined.
6. Problem-solving methodology is administered.
7. Assignments result from the studies.
8. Results are posted.
9. Celebration of results.

One blow-molding plastics company in Baltimore routinely institutes a two-hour refresher problem-solving course for all team members each time a new problem-solving team is charged with an improvement task. This can refer to data accuracy task teams or any other process improvement activity. This has led to the improved use of the tools and more repeatable methodology from team to team. The sessions are facilitated by the team sponsor, usually the supervisor or manager of the area where the improvement is being guided. This has a twofold benefit: managers and supervisors become especially comfortable with the tools and they have a much higher expectation of the team using them.

Documentation of the Resulting Process Changes

As the control group methodology and problem-solving tools are put to use, solutions become apparent and are assigned and implemented. These process improvement solutions must be apparent through procedures documented appropriately. This closes the loop on sustainable performance, something that is necessary if you do not want to have to go through the same problem-solving exercise next year! This is actually the theory behind ISO (International Organization for Standardization) logic.

Documentation of decisions made is the first step in the process of having these decisions become policy and procedures. Without documentation, it is unlikely that these decisions will govern future behavior consistently. These documents are also the basis for training that will be so important for process control.

As Bruce Jones, project manager at a urethane-extruding manufacturer in central Massachusetts, says, "A process or procedure solution without a document is a *soft* solution. *Hard* solutions require documentation."

> "**A** process or procedure solution without a document is a *soft* solution. *Hard* solutions require documentation."
>
> Bruce Jones

The next chapter will deal specifically with documentation.

Taking a Physical Inventory

For many companies beginning their journey to inventory record accuracy, a complete wall-to-wall physical inventory will be appropriate once accurate control groups show that process controls are in place (Figure 5-4). This is particularly the case for companies starting out with very low levels of data integrity. Although it is virtually impossible to count a wall-

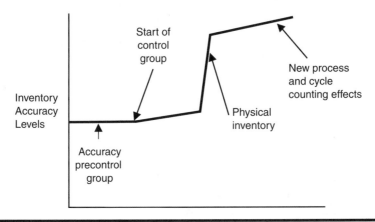

Figure 5-4. Effects of the physical inventory after the control group has eliminated errors.

to-wall inventory at 100 percent accuracy, it can be a significant improvement as a starting point for the cycle counting process to begin. The good news is that this is the last physical inventory the company will have to take!

Eliminating the Physical Inventory Forever

It is the control group (determination of root cause and eliminating each root cause) that allows the effective use of a one-last-time physical inventory. The control group methodology is arguably the most important phase in the 120-day process of achieving inventory record accuracy. It is in these first few days that change begins, allowing the new habits of predictable, repeatable high performance to be established. Without the control group, it is very difficult to really understand where the variation is coming from and even more difficult to determine what actions should be taken. Strict use of the control group with proper resulting process improvement should forever greatly reduce inventory surprises and/or the associated high costs of expediting and arranging for and funding priority freight costs.

Once a robust process is in place to ensure accuracy, the physical inventory normally done annually can also be eliminated. The annual physical inventory is not a value-added exercise. Like inspecting quality into a process, which has long been known as the least-effective method of assuring quality, the physical inventory is really designed to ensure and fix balance accuracy issues. Since it is impossible to count perfectly, especially in a massive factory- or warehouse-wide effort, it also can cause some problems that did not exist prior to the count.

At The Raymond Corporation's remanufacturing and aftermarket parts distribution center in Syracuse, New York, there is no annual physical because of confirmed accuracy of inventory location balances. However, the external auditor still requires a confirmation each year. This is normally a statistically correct sample of at least 300 location balances to be confirmed. The management team does the counts as requested by the external auditor each year end. After the sample counts are completed, the results of the requested counts are handed over to the auditors, but no internal checks are made to the computer records and no updates are transacted to the perpetual records. What is the reason for this lack of action resulting from the count?

The Raymond Corporation knows that it is very difficult to count 300 locations at once in a mass effort and have it be absolutely accurate. By simply handing in the results and not making any internal comparisons and transactions, any inaccuracies from the count are not reflected in the perpetual balances. The company's confidence in its ability to maintain balance accuracy on an everyday level is higher than its confidence to mass count location balances accurately! This is the level of confidence every warehouse and factory should have!

In another example, a factory in North Carolina that manufactures appliances also has a high confidence level in its inventory balances. Recently, not realizing the liabilities associated with massive counts, it did a physical inventory required by its European headquarters and updated its perpetual records as most companies normally do in this situation. The result was a degradation of its balance accuracy that showed up in the subsequent normal random cycle counts the week following the physical inventory. In this specific case, accuracy dropped by more than seven percentage points because of the inaccuracies contributed by the physical wall-to-wall count.

Many organizations in the U.S. believe that the elimination of the physical inventory count once a year is not possible due to imaginary laws or regulations. (It is a fact that almost all high-performance organizations in the U.S. legally and ethically do not schedule and execute an annual wall-to-wall physical inventory.) There are some countries that do have regulations governing the requirement and in that case there is no choice.

The annual wall-to-wall physical inventory is not a value-added activity in high-performance organizations. Sometimes it can even degrade accuracy.

In companies where regulation requires the count, there is not usually a regulation requiring the updating of the perpetual records postcount.

These lessons and others assure organizations that good process pays back in real dollars and is worth the effort and time spent to establish disciplined practices and procedures. The savings come from many sources and can be very large.

6

Day 8–45:
Policies and Standard Operating Procedures, The Training Tools for Process Control

Day 8 through 45 and beyond
Some procedures may already be developed by day 8 and documentation can begin. Document each procedure as it is developed. Documentation is not only important for data accuracy; it is the essence of agreement for all of the facility processes.

Reason for Documentation

In most organizations, predictable repeatable data integrity requires a change in habits. This change must be administered consistently with repeatable procedures if this change is to develop into maintained and sustained change.

No one likes the notion of adding paperwork to any operation or transaction, but as data accuracy and repeatability of process become the target, documentation becomes necessary. Without written agreement, humans tend to remember things differently. This is historically true in everything from land boundary disputes to factory transaction procedures.

If two people in a room agree on a process rule, each leaves the room with an idea of what the agreement was. Each of the players has an experience filter through which they listen to process discussions. Because of these filters, the interpretation of the agreement can and often will vary. Therein lies the need for documentation.

Without documentation, procedures can deviate and evolve in a direction unrelated to the original objectives of the process. The purpose of documentation is to perform the following value-added advantages.

To Provide Consistency in the Business

The documentation of processes by itself does little to increase consistency. The combined efforts of auditing and insisting that documentation be correct are the vehicles that instill consistency in the manufacturing cycle. The objective should be repeatability of a process with predictability of performance. This applies to the objectives of inventory record accuracy.

Many companies pursue ISO (International Organization for Standardization) certification for exactly that reason. The ISO standard is a globally accepted manufacturing consistency standard originally made widely known by business organizations in Europe and suppliers to European companies. ISO structure and discipline can provide the necessary infrastructure to control and audit documentation and procedures for consistency. In an ISO environment, the data accuracy procedures developed from the inventory record accuracy initiative can fit appropriately into the ISO process of controlling documentation, although ISO certification is certainly not a prerequisite to accuracy. This internationally recognized standard has been adopted by many companies worldwide. Done properly, many such companies find at least the standardized ISO format for procedures helpful in their quest for data integrity. *Done properly* is the key phrase! There are many organizations that have been ISO certified that have not yet achieved Class A levels of inventory accuracy, so do not confuse the two designations. ISO certification normally depends more on the process documentation matching the process execution. If the intent of the documentation in your ISO implementation is to have robust transaction discipline and is designed accordingly, the resulting balances will be accurate. This obviously does not negate the need for a control group, root cause analysis, and a management system.

To Gain Control of the Processes

In most businesses, changing the culture of an organization is a significant and challenging undertaking. When people hold certain ideals as important in their lives, these ideals begin to impact their surroundings. This relates to certain expectations in consistency and predictability. For example, in some businesses, expediting that includes shortcuts and behaviors that skip steps can be perceived as good behavior, even rewarded in some cases. In many of these organizations, a good understanding of the process and procedure is inadequate, creating a lack of concern for the steps in the procedure.

In one manufacturing business in upstate New York, a thirty-year veteran employee of a particular plant built his reputation on being the best in the business at "saving the day." He had honed the expediting process to the point that others, including management, relied on him to "come through" in a pinch when it was necessary. The normal modus operandi of this individual was to shortcut the system every chance he could in the name of speed and customer service. He actually was rewarded many times for exactly the behaviors we are attempting to eliminate with the processes in this book. For example, when parts were being expedited from suppliers, he would often authorize a partial shipment and not complete the receiving transaction properly. This left the open purchase order file with order quantities that were not accurate.

> **M**any organizations going through this change find that there is a percentage of people who simply cannot make the change and are either eventually asked or ask themselves to "get off the train" because it is moving too fast.

A new CEO came to the organization with an objective to cut costs through a renewed effort in process excellence and disciplines. Shortly after he arrived, a bright light began to shine on the shortcuts and the costs incurred by the organization over time. The result from this new focus included new procedure documentation, training, and policing of transactions. This is a cultural change that greatly affected the style of the shortcut hero described earlier at this company. He went from hero to villain over night. While this is not the objective of a focus on discipline, it needs to be considered as the dynamics of behavior are changed. People need to understand not only what the emphasis is, but why. Clear understanding allows these same people to determine the needed changes themselves instead of having the new procedures simply dictated to them by what they see as an outsider who has not been through the same war. In this case, the gentleman was able to understand and change his habits and took a job in purchasing negotiating prices and contracts with suppliers. The stories do not all end this happily, however. Organizational culture is not to be taken lightly.

Process Mapping

Documentation plays a part in this transition. If a department or division manager has no real detailed understanding of a specific process, he or she is at the mercy of the people who hold the knowledge base. While this may seem reasonable to some, it can put a business in a very precarious position.

Process mapping, the methodology of documenting the steps and flow of a process using symbols, is an effective tool for pictorially representing the "is condition" of the current process as well as visually describing the desired procedure. Process maps can add value. Gaining control over a business requires an understanding of the processes as they exist today. Documentation allows for this understanding and creates the baseline for improvement. In organizations where management understands the benefits of documentation, process maps always provide great value.

As the group goes through the exercise of mapping a process, people are forced to think about the inputs and outputs of each step. These linkages affect other procedures and, accordingly, the resulting benefits to the overall organization. In many cases, the documenting of the "is condition" reveals procedures that (unknowingly) negatively affect others in line for process handoffs.

Process mapping is a relatively easy tool to learn and with practice can be done at almost any level in the organization as procedures are shored up for accuracy and predictability. Figure 6-1 is a simple process map of a stockroom-type procedure.

Training Guides

Training is the third common use or value of process mapping and documentation of processes. One major responsibility of standard operating procedures (SOPs) is to verbalize or document the process maps. Once the process is documented correctly, showing all of the decision points in

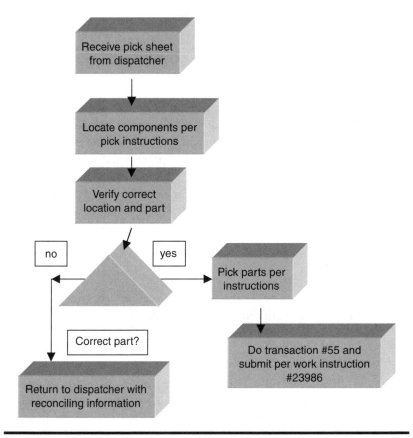

Figure 6-1. Sample process map.

flowchart form, it can easily be turned into a training document. This is done simply by writing down the actions and decisions made during the process as described in the process map. The result of this is an SOP that describes not only why but how certain functions are performed.

There is, of course, more to the SOP than just the verbalization of the process map. Additionally, there are other necessary information or communication items that are helpful in achieving global understanding and acknowledgment. These communication items usually include boundaries of scope, expected outcome or objective of the procedure (sometimes referred to as "deliverables"), tools required, performance metrics associated with the procedure, a listing of other related SOPs, samples of documents used in the process, author(s), authorization(s), and date last reviewed. More detail on best-of-class SOP format follows later in this chapter.

To Enable Continuous Improvement

Of the four purposes of documentation listed here, enabling continuous improvement is the most important. Once the organization becomes process oriented, opportunity is evaluated in terms of waste elimination or process variation reduction as it applies to process and procedure. Each step in the current "is condition" can be evaluated to determine if it adds value to the process. Continuous improvement results from simplification efforts to move the process toward the "should be" condition. The expectation should include a procedural review at least every six months. This means every document must be reviewed every six months. If this is done regularly, most organizations find that they do not have too many to review each day. If each process owner reviews their own documentation, it is a fairly efficient process. Often the review requirement is no more than having to review a few procedures each month.

Accessibility

Obviously, computers and system networking have had a major impact on business processes today. These tools are helping take time out of processes and aiding in the reduction of customer service cycle times through efficiency gains. In many cases, accuracy is impacted positively. Because of this exciting positive effect, more and more applications for computers are being developed daily. Most businesses today are networked through connected hardware and software tools. This allows the opportunity to have SOPs accessible to all who are on the network. While this may seem adequate, maybe even advantageous, be reminded that the limitation of this practice is the accessibility of the system.

People on the factory floor or in the warehouse need access to SOPs just as frequently as do the office personnel. If the culture is to know the procedure and follow it, access must be easy for all. Many companies have a complete hard copy set of all procedures available in a central location (such as the lunchroom) for people who might not have access to the computer net-

Factory personnel need access to documentation such as procedures and policies just as much as office workers and management do.

work system. If the cafeteria does not lend itself as a good reference library location, other special documentation areas can be established in the factory or warehouse. This centralized and well-advertised location is also a good place to have company policy documents accessible, such as human resource practices and policies affecting employees.

If documents are available in hard copy form as described, a procedure also must be instituted to provide for the timely placement of procedures when they are revised. The format and procedural review typically associated with an ISO certification can provide a guideline for review and revision.

Written Procedures

Standard Operating Procedures

It is recommended that as documentation is initiated in an organization, a standard format be adopted. If your organization has done work in ISO requirements, you are already familiar with this requirement. Having a template supports consistency and makes sure that all the desired elements are resident in each procedural document. The following topics are reasonably complete (see also Figures 6-2 through 6-5 for examples) and should be included in a well-written SOP template.

Define the Boundaries or Scope

The art of process documentation includes sensitivity for linkages to other aspects of the process or business. Each process and corresponding SOP has a reason for existence. The SOP should refer to other SOPs that address linkages and dependencies. These linkages identify waste opportunities.

By the same token, it should be noted in the SOP that connecting processes are linked with the output of the process described. For every process, there should be a driver/cause and a result/effect. Again, it is this cause-and-effect relationship understanding that will enable a team of educated employees to convert opportunities into business improvement.

Many companies connect these processes visually. Using string, they attach each process to the wall of a conference room as it was documented. They then connect the effects to causes. When completed, all four walls are usually decorated with the complex process of order fulfillment in the

Title **Inventory Balance Accuracy Metric**   SOP# 022531
Process owner and authorizer **Bill Doe**
Approved by **Jim Green**
Last revision or review 14 **July xxxx**
Author **Jane Smith**   Page **1 of 2**

1. Boundaries or Scope
Starts with xxxxxxxxxxxxxxxxxxxxxxxxxxxxxxxxxxxxxxxxxxxxxx
Ends with   xxxxxxxxxxxxxxxxxxxxxxxxxxxxxxxxxxxxxxxxxxxxxx

2. Why this procedure exists
xxxxxxxxxxxxxxxxxxxxxxxxxxxxxxxxxxxxxxxxxxxxxxxxxxxxxxx
xxxxxxxxxxxxxxxxxxxxxxxxxxxxxxxxxxxxxxxxxxxxxxxxxxxxxxx

3. Objective of this procedure
xxxxxxxxxxxxxxxxxxxxxxxxxxxxxxxxxxxxxxxxxxxxxxxxxxxxxxx
xxxxxxxxxxxxxxxxxxxxxxxxxxxxxxxxxxxxxxxxxxxxxxxxxxxxxxx

4. Measurement Process
    1) xxxxxxxxxxxxxxxxxxxxxxxxxxxxxxxxxxxxxxxxxxxxxx
    2) xxxxxxxxxxxxxxxxxxxxxxxxxxxxxxxxxxxxxxxxxxxxxx
    3) xxxxxxxxxxxxxxxxxxxxxxxxxxxxxxxxxxxxxxxxxxxxxx

Figure 6-2.   Inventory procedure, page 1.

facility. It also becomes obvious where the holes in the process are and where linkages to existing processes reside. Visualizing it may help to appreciate mapping as a powerful tool. Once this exercise has been completed, the definitions of scope or boundaries of the SOP are stated more easily. By defining these boundaries, it becomes easier to train and audit the procedure later.

The wording to accomplish the scope might simply state: "The procedure starts with the generation of a pick requirement in the MRP system and ends with the actual movement of material from the stockroom to production." A list of related SOPs would be referenced for process linkage.

Describe Why the Procedure Exists

Describing why the procedure exists can be accomplished in the objective statement and does not necessarily have to be a separate paragraph in the

Title **Inventory Balance Accuracy Metric**   SOP# 022531
Process owner and authorizer **Bill Doe**
Approved by **Jim Green**
Last revision or review 14 **July xxxx**
Author **Jane Smith**   Page 2 of 2

5. **Measurement Equation**

$$\frac{\text{Number of locations correct}}{\text{Number of locations checked}} \times 100 = \% \text{ Posted}$$

6. **Reporting Process**

xxxxxxxxxxxxxxxxxxxxxxxxxxxxxxxxxxxxxxxxxxxxxxxxxxxxxxx
xxxxxxxxxxxxxxxxxxxxxxxxxxxxxxxxxxxxxxxxxxxxxxxxxxxxxxx

7. **Other Related Procedures**
    SOP 485906 Transaction Matrix
    SOP 051384 Procedure for Picking Standard Kits
    SOP 940569 Weekly Performance Review

Figure 6-3. Inventory procedure, page 2.

SOP. If this definition is missing, too many times the procedure can be misunderstood and manipulated for totally different purposes. The explanation of why the process exists is often an opportunity for further improvement.

An example of good definition follows. It takes place in a multiplant environment with baked ice-cream cones as the main product. Master scheduling in this environment was exercised from a central organization. As this process was mapped, the duplication of effort became very obvious — there were redundant steps for material and capacity checks being exercised. Because there were decisions being made with inaccurate data, this redundancy was required. As the company drove to higher levels of database accuracy, processes needed to be changed to get the full benefits of the data quality improvement. By mapping the process, the opportunity to eliminate waste became obvious and could be changed quickly.

The procedure document in this company stated: "The reason this global master scheduling procedure document exists is to ensure the consistent and predictable execution of schedules in our organization and

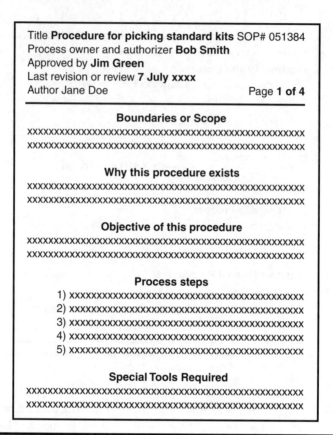

Figure 6-4.   Picking procedure, page 1.

"The reason this global master scheduling procedure document exists is to ensure the consistent and predictable execution of schedules and to ensure that no cost-added or unnecessary duplication of effort is incorporated into our process."

to ensure that no cost added or unnecessary duplication of effort is incorporated into our master scheduling process."

It was in evaluating the master scheduling process worldwide, through both reviewing procedures and mapping the process, that much duplication was discovered. The result of this exercise was fewer operations in the scheduling process and more central control, as was desired. The process became more flexible and responsive to customer need as all of the order management was done from the central location as well.

Title **Procedure for picking standard kits**   SOP# 051384

Page **2 of 4**

Performance measures

Reference SOP# 071452, Inventory location balance
accuracy performance measurement.

Reference documentation linked to SOP# 051384

Reference SOP# 101089, Warehouse transactions
Reference SOP# 875634, Weekly Performance
ReviewReference Work Instruction # 87657, Downloading
picktransactions

Documents attached to this procedure

Process map for SOP# 051384
Sample pick sheet, document # 90897

Figure 6-5. Picking procedure, page 2.

Describe the Objective or Deliverable

Describing why a procedure exists (step above) and describing what the deliverable is are two different things. Both help to lock the spirit of the procedure for the future in case of interpretation. The deliverable should be measurable. An example might be in an intracompany environment; a bill of lading SOP for internal transports (plant to plant) might be: "To provide proper documentation for all shipments between divisions in different geographic locations, to provide accurate and timely visibility to material control analysts and accounting personnel of intracompany material movement." By listing the objective, the author is tested as to whether the objective is worthwhile and is given expectations on how to verify if the procedure is working properly.

List the Steps in the Process

List the process steps in order. Capture all decision points and alternatives that are in the procedure in real life. It is these alternatives and decision points that give the SOP the real instructional value. This should quickly remind you of the previous discussion on process mapping. In this section, many organizations actually attach a process map to best fulfill this documentation requirement.

How many times have you wanted to know something about a software application and found the "help" tool to be of no help at all because this particular feature or option has been left out of the instructions? Have several team members review the list for accuracy on completion of the draft.

As an example, the following list of steps refers back to the sample process map (Figure 6-1).

> **Step 1**. Receive pick sheet from dispatcher. The pick sheet will have the assembly item number, the customer order number, a list of each component required in the assembly, pick codes, unit of measure, and quantities for each item.
>
> **Step 2.** Locate components with pick code other than "L". Note that pick code "L" is a line storage item and will not be required in the kit being picked.
>
> **Step 3**. Verify each part as the bin is approached. Check for the right part per the description, adequate quantity, and the right location. Check to see that there are no foreign parts mixed in the location. All parts with the same part number should look alike.
>
> IF PART, QUANTITY, AND LOCATION ARE CORRECT proceed with Step 4. IF NOT, proceed to Step 3a.
>
> **Step 3a.** If there is any discrepancy in the part or location of the required part, note the information and mark the pick sheet "not completed due to _____ (reason)." Go on to the next pick sequence, or if this is the last pick sheet you have, return to the dispatcher. Always place any incomplete pick sheets with proper explanations on the top of the pile of sheets handed in to the dispatcher.
>
> **Step 4.** Pick parts per instructions concerning unit of measure, quantity, and correct part. Be mindful that some parts may still be stored in boxes with multiple parts in the box that are not clearly identified. When a kit is completed with no deviations from instructions, hit the red "complete" mushroom-shaped button on the fork truck. This instructs the dispatcher where you are in the pick cycle and also sets the software to relieve inventory balances. Do not hit the red

"complete" mushroom button if there were any deviations from the pick ticket. If you experienced any picking deviations as compared to the original pick sheet, move to Step 5.

Step 5 (to be used with pick exceptions). When all pick sheets are complete from the picking cycle of one run, return to the dispatch area and download your system transactions per work instruction 23986. This will automatically transact the kit components from location balances. If not at the end of the shift, proceed back to dispatch area for next picking instruction.

SPECIAL NOTE: If in the middle of a pick at the end of the shift, finish the component part being worked on and note on the pick sheet status of pick. No transactions are necessary at this point. The next shift will finish the pick run and complete the transactions per work instruction 23986.

List Special Tools Required

This list of "special tools" would normally include items required for the successful completion of the procedure. In a warehouse, these might include items such as a computer terminal, software tools, fixtures, chain sling, forklift truck, scales, special measuring equipment, gauges, etc. This also helps to eliminate nonrequired instruments/tools from the specific area.

It can be interesting to audit the tool section of procedures when doing 5-S housekeeping and workplace organization exercises. If it is not in the documentation, ask if it is needed. If so, update the SOP; if not, get rid of it!

Reference Performance Measurements

Most processes should have *at least* one performance measurement assuring process control. Work instructions and/or material conversion processes also might have quality standards as performance measurements and/or efficiency measurements.

The SOP should include a definition of that measurement process and, if available, a cross-reference to the SOP that defines the measurement in detail if it is not described in the procedure itself. If applicable, an example of the measurement calculation also should be attached. This is a very important element of procedures that is often left out. The measurement makes auditing very easy and can lead to early detection of noncompliance.

For example, a warehouse picking procedure (SOP) might reference the inventory accuracy performance measurement SOP. In this referenced document, the calculation and ownership for inventory record accuracy would be clearly defined, as would the reporting expectations.

Reference Other SOPs or Work Instructions That Pertain or Connect to This Process

If there are other SOPs or pertinent documents that have linkages to the current SOP, they should be referenced by a document control number. This is typically quite common, especially if the processes have defined inputs and outputs as discussed in this chapter.

For example, an intracompany bill of lading procedure most likely would reference additional procedures such as "loading over the road trucks," "accessing the computer system," or "receiving material into shipping" procedures. These are procedures that would be connected through inputs and outputs or cause and effect. In the conference room case described earlier, where string was used to connect processes visually, these are the procedures that would be connected, one to the other.

The control number is the identifier that separates this document from others and allows the user lookup capability when required.

Attach Sample Documents and/or Sample Computer Screens

Many processes have control documents and/or computer screens that are used in the procedure. Make sure both are referenced in the procedure and have examples attached in the form of pictures or graphics. This requires a serial number or control number to be assigned to each document. This serial number would be found on both the procedure and the attached referenced document. When these are logged into a database, referencing becomes an especially powerful tool. For example, when changes or updates are being made to a procedure, having full reference to related documents helps ensure complete process revision integrity.

Determine Who Wrote the Document

Knowing the author of a specific procedure can be extremely helpful when clarification is required. If more than one person was involved, the one responsible for the process itself should be referenced. Avoid multiple names in this section. Process ownership is important for proper account-ability. The author is often the process owner or a delegate of the process owner.

Determine Who Authorized the Document

The authorizing signature is important for controlling the variability in the overall process. SOPs should not be changed at random or by people who do not understand the impact on other parts of the organization or overall process. The authorizing signature should be someone with direct knowl-edge and authority over the area addressed by the procedure. This would normally be the inventory manager or materials manager in inventory control procedures.

In some organizations, the plant manager signs all procedures as a sign of support for required disciplines. While the spirit of this decision is valid, the realities of the effectiveness can be questionable. Having the plant manager sign numerous authoriza-tions without really knowing the process in question is not a value-added activity and should be avoided. Many times in these in-stances, the plant manager does not even read them; he or she takes the word of the author. This does not necessarily contribute to a value-added process.

> **W**hen top managers (such as plant managers) sign off on all pro-cedures and rarely read them, it is probably not a value-added pro-cess. The process owners should be accountable for most of these authorizations.

Date Written

The date that the SOP was written should be a required field for reference purposes. This can help with investigations and audit trails. This date does not change even as the SOP is updated and revised.

Date Last Audited

Procedures should be audited on a regular basis. This means that just as a company might audit the financial records, inventory record accuracy or manufacturing bill of material accuracy procedures also should be audited. The date in this field should reflect the last time the procedure was verified as accurate. It does not mean that there is an expectation to change every procedure every six months. It does mean procedures are audited for accuracy on a timely basis.

What many companies do is post a verification audit for every procedure every six months. The process owner is responsible for this audit, and if no changes are required, he or she simply signifies process accuracy and the audited date is revised. If this is done regularly, most process owners will have only a few each week to look at and it does not become insurmountable to keep up with. If, on the other hand, it is ignored until the end of the year, or there is an expectation that all SOPs will be reviewed in a short time frame, it can become a nightmare to achieve.

Who Should Write the Documentation?

The most successful documentation initiatives use people involved in the actual processes to determine the documentation mapping and verbiage. It ends up being more accurate and, because the learning that happens from the exercise is invaluable, the company process experts should do the documentation. The real benefits will surface as the SOPs, especially the process map components, are put to use.

> Some organizations use temporary help to write the procedures. If it is not worth the time for the process owners and their reports, the value will be minimized.

Some organizations use temporary outside help or find someone to become the expert and document all processes rather than utilizing the people involved. This method often ends up with little internal ownership of the documentation and little internal awareness or learning from the process.

There are generic SOPs available in the market from various sources. In the case of the better ones, these do add value, but they do not take the place of proper documentation. Used effectively, these become a process outline for documentation and a reminder of the core documents that are necessary. They can save time, but in every case, to make them effective they must be updated for each specific application. As the saying goes, "there is no free lunch."

In terms of documentation requirements, it usually seems like there is never a good time to devote the time and resources to go through process analysis to create detailed documentation. It is not necessarily the most exciting project on the list, but it is one that is necessary for the sustainability of inventory accuracy. Most successful organizations simply prioritize this activity as important and schedule the time to get the needed documentation accomplished.

Process Mapping

The discussion to this point has dealt with the most familiar part of documentation — the written procedures. The exercise of drawing the map with all the decisions, steps, and alternatives is faster, more efficient, easier, and can even be more accurate as decision points are easily clarified in process maps.

When preparing for a process-mapping exercise, people who are involved in the process should prepare ahead of time by writing down a summary of activities performed within the boundaries of the planned process map. They also should be instructed to be aware of any documents or written procedures that affect their part of the process. By bringing these to the session, two things happen: first, people will be encouraged to think about the process, especially as it relates to defining policies and practices, and second, time can be saved in the discussion phase later.

The group assigned to this task should be kept to a manageable size. Usually six to eight or fewer participants is appropriate. Obviously, the facilitation is easiest with fewer people, but depending on the level of problem-solving skills, this rule may be a guideline only. Complexity of the process being mapped is also a factor. Sometimes it is necessary to have support personnel, such as accounting or engineering, as team members for the exercise.

Once the team is prepared and assembled to begin the mapping exercise, a facilitator should once again define the boundaries of the exercise. This would include defining the starting point. An example might be: "The process map will begin from the point at which a pick list is generated by the computer system and the picked parts are transacted against to decrease the location balances for the parts picked" (see Figure 6-6). A good way to make this clear is to actually put labels representing these starting and ending points on the conference room wall (yellow sticky pad type), one on the far left side and one on the far right side.

From this point forward, it is recommended that the team continue using the sticky yellow pieces of paper. (No significance to the color other than that is the most widely recognized color for sticky note pads.) These "sticky notes" are easily moved when it is realized that a step was missed

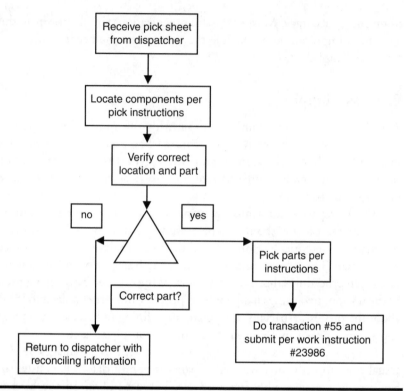

Figure 6-6. Picking process map.

in defining the flow and needs to be added. This popular method makes the documentation process very flexible. Adding newly recognized, but omitted, linked processes can easily be facilitated this way. As the team progresses, the exercise will begin to develop a "picture" of the process/ procedure as it exists today. Since the objective is to get reasonably detailed, this sticky note method can be very helpful. Changes and updates to the process "picture" will continue throughout the exercise.

Often an unexpected deliverable from this process analysis is the resulting improvements that become obvious as the steps are acknowledged on paper. When this exercise is done with sincere rigor, it is rare that improvements are not discovered and implemented. Unless the review has team effort that is serious about getting value from the documentation, it will not bring maximum value to the table.

The previous examples (Figures 6-1 and 6-6) used earlier in this book are good, yet simple, examples of process maps that would be attached to an SOP. The extent of the process map depends totally on the definition of the process boundaries. Actual examples could be much more detailed as required.

Documentation Control

Once documentation is created and processes are defined properly and are being executed, revision control must also become a priority. Similar to the requirements of engineering change control, management must provide tight accuracy and effectivity controls on SOPs. This control is necessary to protect the investment that has been made in understanding, improving, and documenting the process maps and procedures of the organization's activities.

Documentation control should be kept simple. Process owners, the people who are responsible for the particular process described by the document, are the "managers or controllers" of change within that process. This puts the process owner in the position of auditing, updating, authorizing, and communicating process details and controls defined by an SOP. Document control becomes part of the oversight requirements of the process owners. A document control procedure would typically include the process to deal with the submission of ideas pertaining to improvements, investigation, and/or testing of new process designs, procedure authorization, revision communication, training when required, and finally filing of the revised method. The document control process itself should have a written procedure to limit variability in this important process.

Process owners should be in charge of the process audits of their own documents. This distributes the workload reasonably and allows solid background knowledge in the auditing process.

All individuals directly involved in the procedures should be trained in document control procedures just as they are trained in the respective processes.

Each procedure and map should have a control number assigned. The control number, along with the initiation, revision, or audit date, acts as the revision-sequencing tool. As they are replaced by newer procedure revisions, previous procedures should be discarded to eliminate confusion.

Hard copy can be less intimidating for factory personnel and often is more readily utilized. It is just easier to get at.

Keep the documentation accessible to all employees. By locating the procedures and maps either centrally or in several accessible areas, workers are encouraged to verify procedures and reconcile actual to planned process. Many organizations locate documentation in the cafeteria or in some central location set up specifically for employees in the factory and warehouse. Hard copy is often easiest for employees to access quickly and can be less intimidating.

Title **Policy for Employee Purchases**   POL# HR7865

Process owner and authorizer **Mary Smith**

Approved by **Jim Green**

Last revision or review 25 Feb **xxxx**

Author **Jim Brown**   Page **1 of 1**

1. Why this policy exists

xxxxxxxxxxxxxxxxxxxxxxxxxxxxxxxxxxxxxxxxxxxxxxxxxxxxx
xxxxxxxxxxxxxxxxxxxxxxxxxxxxxxxxxxxxxxxxxxxxxxxxxxxxx

2. Objective of this policy

xxxxxxxxxxxxxxxxxxxxxxxxxxxxxxxxxxxxxxxxxxxxxxxxxxxxx
xxxxxxxxxxxxxxxxxxxxxxxxxxxxxxxxxxxxxxxxxxxxxxxxxxxxx

3. Policy Statement

xxxxxxxxxxxxxxxxxxxxxxxxxxxxxxxxxxxxxxxxxxxxxxxxxxxxx
xxxxxxxxxxxxxxxxxxxxxxxxxxxxxxxxxxxxxxxxxxxxxxxxxxxxx

4. To Purchase Company Materials refer to
SOP# 042930. Employee Purchases.

Figure 6-7.   Policy example.

Policies

There are three levels of documentation in most businesses:

1. Policies
2. Procedures
3. Work instructions

Procedures describe the specific requirements of a process, whereas policies dictate the parameters within management's rules for the business (see the sample in Figure 6-7). Examples of policy documentation affecting inventory accuracy could include policies such as employee purchase of company inventory or distribution of samples for customers. There are many such possible policies.

Summary

Documentation is an important prerequisite to process control. Starting on day 15, procedure decisions should be documented in the form of standardized documentation. Normally, improvements are already starting as procedures are being shored up. These tools help improve record accuracy by creating a common understanding of processes, provide a map for training, and provide a base for continuous improvement. High-performance companies respect the need for such process definition and document control.

7

Day 9:
Inventory Organization
and Storage Patterns

Day 9
Begin determining the desired inventory organization and storage layout.

Introduction

Determining the optimum storage layout is not a job that starts by day 9 and ends on any specific day. Instead, this topic is one that starts by day 9 and never ends as process improvements are incorporated into the inventory flow model. Every time the cycle time is shortened or the product is redesigned, flow layout can be affected. Linkages to process improvement as well as availability of capital to rearrange new methods all contribute to the timing.

It is unacceptable in most applications to have factory-wide location labels. Items can get lost too easily and it is virtually impossible to know where everything is.

The main storage organization requirement in establishing accurate inventory location balances is to have inventory stored logically, neat and organized. This means locations (labeled designated storage areas) cannot be sized as vaguely as "factory." This vague location label can create

difficulties in finding inventory when it is needed for production requirements and makes cycle counting almost impossible as you attempt to
confirm accuracy in test counts. The cycle count personnel in an environment with no location designations are never sure if they have counted the
entire inventory. When does the cycle counter stop looking — when he or
she finds the quantity recorded in the perpetual records? That is what some
misguided organizations do.

A couple of years ago, a manufacturing plant in France was ready to
launch a new software system, but had no real meaningful location designations loaded to the system. Its locations were all designated as one
"general" location that, in effect, simply filled the location field in the
system. There was no warehouse or factory map that could show where this
location could be found. In effect, this meant that the locations were as
large as the plant. While this may be seen by some as simplification of
process, in a plant like this one, which was over 600,000 square feet,
without knowing the location of inventory, there was no foolproof way to
verify its accuracy or locate materials easily.

The only sane way to know where inventory is and to be able to verify
count accuracy is to have locations designated that relate to specific areas
within the plant. Location size and design will be covered later in more
detail.

Factories or distribution facilities that have inventory stored by process
design or practice for more than twenty-four hours and/or that want to net
inventory balances against planned
or actual requirements should have
the capability to audit and verify
inventory balance accuracy. Auditing inventory accuracy in the previous example would require searching the entire plant, every corner,
aisle, rack, and cabinet drawer to
reconcile accuracy. *Bonne chance*
(French for "good luck")! This is
not a problem foreign to any soil. Companies trying to shortcut good
processes or companies not in full understanding of lean manufacturing
techniques (also referred to as just in time) will often neglect the need for
good, organized, and accessible storage techniques linked to their planning
system.

> **T**wenty-four-hour rule — Any in-
> ventory that is, by system design
> or by habit, kept in one area for
> more than twenty-four hours regu-
> larly should be logged into the
> inventory control system by item,
> location, and quantity.

In any facility where inventory is resident for more than twenty-four
hours, there should be locations sized with the process in mind. Addition-

ally, this inventory should be defined as a controlled area and one that has transactions defining the boundaries of this balance. This can be done through kanban controls or more traditional receipt and issue transactions. In this chapter, there will be more color offered around the rules used by high-performance organizations.

The Beginning Checklist for Organization

Experience says that regardless of the goal, understanding the final vision with clarity around that goal always helps keep the journey on track. It can also make the journey more efficient by minimizing false starts. Using this logic, the vision or list of steps to address organized storage would include the following important topics.

Good Housekeeping/Workplace Organization

Good housekeeping is a basic rule that should be understood as a prerequisite to any good system discipline. Good housekeeping in a stores area includes having all material in its place and a place for all materials. Lines on the floor designate storage areas for specific items, racks are well labeled and only materials intended for the locations are in them, and material is moved in a timely basis. As you read this, take a mental inventory of your warehouse. Are you proud of the housekeeping throughout your facility where inventory is controlled and stored?

In high-performance organizations, pallets are in very close alignment. They are not allowed to extend into the aisle from racks (see Figure 7-1). While some may think this unnecessary, this type of standard helps both safety as well as attention to neatness.

It is also important to have proper receptacles for waste such as steel or plastic strapping or other banding or packaging materials, including unwanted skids. These receptacles must be both sized properly and located in areas where they are needed. Sometimes this means waste receptacles on the forklift trucks.

Sufficient Lighting

Lighting may seem like a pretty obvious need, but many organizations ignore it. Sometimes this is a result of racks being constructed in areas not initially designed for storage. For example, it could happen that as a business grows, storage racks are added in adjoining areas years after

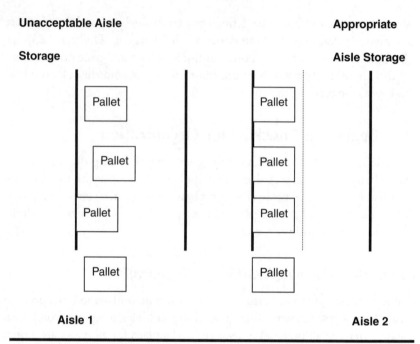

Figure 7-1. Aisle alignment.

lighting has been installed with another initial purpose in mind for the space. The result is often heavy shadows in the exact spaces where high accuracy of picks is expected. This is especially important where small parts are stored or where items can be very similar in size and configuration, but have different item numbers.

Obviously, when designing the lighting in your storage areas, do not forget material handling access. Lights cannot hang down where lift truck masts must be able to maneuver. When starting to evaluate storage patterns, it is good to take a walking tour through the storage areas with the sole purpose of evaluating proper lighting.

Properly Sized Locations

Locations should be the right size for the purpose and process. Locations that are too big make it easy for parts to be mixed together. Mixing different parts in the same location makes pick accuracy less foolproof and should be avoided if at all possible.

Loc 1A1	Loc 1A2	Loc 1A3	Loc 1A4
Loc 1B1	Loc 1B2	Loc 1B3	Loc 1B4
Loc 1C1	Loc 1C2	Loc 1C3	Loc 1C4

Figure 7-2. Using the "chicken coop" divider to a single pallet space.

An example of a common misuse of storage facilities is to have multiple small parts stored in a rack within a single pallet location. In this particular example, if you have many small parts and only pallet racking in the desired storage area, a better way is to divide the pallet space up into smaller "chicken coop"–type spaces using simple plywood dividers (Figure 7-2). These dividers are not expensive and can add percentage points to the record accuracy by eliminating unnecessary errors caused by picking the wrong part from common locations. It can often stop cycle count errors by separating parts into specific locations. This accuracy can often quickly pay for the plywood in eliminated waste associated with inaccurate inventory records such as surprise shortages and poor customer service. Additionally, it can actually promote improved cube management of the space and allow more parts to be stored in the same pallet space.

Many manufacturing or distribution organizations have large, unusual, or odd-shaped parts that have to be stored. A machine tool manufacturer in Ohio has castings that are purchased for the main frame of its large machine tools. These castings are the size of an automobile or larger. Because of variability not yet eliminated in their material flow, these castings have a one-week buffer built into the process. These castings, due to their size, cannot be stored in regular pallet racking, but are not and should not be ignored while addressing the rules for proper storage patterns. In this organization, a storage area is designated with lines painted on the floor for these castings. The large components are neatly lined up and all are accessible by lift truck for the short time they are in storage.

Many organizations have specific needs driven by unusual size or shape restrictions. Most can be solved, and the first step is to address the needs head on. Solutions can range from painted lines on the floor to silos for powdered materials.

Clearly Labeled Drop Areas

In organizations with very lean manufacturing processes, inventory is sometimes pulled through the process by signals, either from location design or a message of some type signaling the next replenishment. When the location design is used, material movement is usually determined by the size of the location — if there is room for material in the location, internal or external suppliers replenish material to the location; if not, no material movement is allowed. This might be a drop area painted on the floor or, in the case of one motorcycle manufacturer, specially designed rolling storage racks only big enough to carry ten sets of handlebars. In this case, when the handlebar racks are full, the assembly of more handlebars is halted until there is an empty rack. This rack is functioning as the kanban signal.

Another similarly designed example is the more familiar "two-bin" system. In this system, like the motorcycle example, bins are sized and available for resupply. When the first bin becomes empty, the assembler signals replenishment by presenting it to the supplier. In some factories, the supplier actually comes into the customer's facility to answer these empty bin signals.

A "two-bin" system can be very simple and useful. When one bin becomes empty, it serves as a sign to replenish. That way, the assembly area never runs out of parts.

These concepts (having limitation on where inventory can be stored) are helpful in all inventory supply applications, not only for the management of material movement but also for accuracy reasons. Most warehouses have material moving in and out regularly throughout some portion of the day. Some high-performance organizations also use the two-bin methodology in another way, to manage put-away. A spe-

Like the warehouse itself, all drop areas should always be clearly marked with painted lines on the floor for appropriate disciplines.

cific area is designated for the receiving drop area with boundaries clearly defined by painted lines on the floor. This area functions as the first bin in the two-bin system. A separate area is also defined as the receiving overflow area. While put-away capacity is aligned with requirements daily, sometimes peak receiving loads require periodic additional capacity. When the receiving backs up to the overflow area, the use of this designated extra space triggers additional resource to the receiving area.

Use of this type of strategy allows documented procedures to cover capacity exception alignment. Supervisors are not required to instruct receiving personnel each time extra capacity is required. It also helps manage the discipline of always having parts in the proper location.

Drop areas should always be specifically outlined. In areas where small parts are stored, this can be a designated, strategically located rack. In organizations where pallets are utilized, it often means lines painted on the floor.

Proper Counting Tools/Methods

Tools, especially high-tech tools, get a lot of publicity when it comes to the topic of data accuracy — and probably way too much credit. While the discipline behind the use of the tools is most often the biggest enabler, nonetheless tools can make the job easier once discipline is in place. There are many types of tools and methods in this category that make discipline easier and help to keep counting and transactions more accurate. The following are a few.

Scales

Scales are often thought of when small parts are counted frequently. This might include items like fasteners, inexpensive hardware, small washers, etc. Small parts are a great application, but there are others as well. Some organizations have raw material in rolls that are very difficult to count or verify. One organization in Ohio makes labels for two-liter beverage bottles. The label film is on rolls and is planned, ordered, and inventoried by the linear foot. Because there is some waste in the start-up operation when feeding film into a printing machine, the usage is not exactly predictable. Therefore the roll is weighed each time it comes back into the warehouse, ensuring accuracy in count within the storeroom walls. This scale is not the typical small bench scale for counting. It is a large floor scale that the forklift and operator can drive across. The weight of the truck and operator is subtracted from the total weight and the balance is converted to feet of film. This ensures record accuracy within the storeroom even in cases where items are hard to count and process usage is somewhat unpredictable. This technique has been used successfully in several different commodity products. It can work with everything from steel to paper rolls.

Logically Sized or Configured Packaging

When items are stored randomly in a bin or pallet, they are especially difficult to count both at pick time and during an audit. Often, items can be placed in packages of ten, twenty-five, or some other helpful number. Computer chips are sometimes stored in static-free tubes with the same amount in each tube. Bearings are often stacked in packaging. This can be very helpful for efficient storage patterns.

> **S**hoppers do not normally count the eggs in an egg carton. They only check them for cracks.

When shoppers go to the store to buy eggs, most do not typically count the eggs in the carton. Many will open the carton to see if there are any cracked eggs, but because of packaging design, it is not necessary to count the eggs. This is not because the shopper does not care whether or not there are twelve eggs, but is because the shopper is assured of this accuracy, even without the audit. This is done simply by looking quickly at the product in the packaging. This technique is also applicable to manufacturing and distribution packaging and can be very helpful in keeping accuracy simple. By having packaging designed like an egg carton, quick observations allow assurance.

Warning: while this multipack strategy is extremely supportive of data accuracy from one perspective, they also comes with a cautionary note. If parts are in multiple packs, as described earlier, they must be clearly labeled on the location as such. The risk in this process comes from pickers who, when instructed to pick ten pieces of an item, pick ten packages! In the case of the egg cartons, most shoppers are well aware that eggs come in dozens. This is not always true with bearings, electrical components, and other manufacturing items not as familiar to the picker as eggs are. This is especially applicable if you have new people picking products.

In some warehouse organizations, the storage bins or pallets are painted red or another bright color for multipacked items only, making them stand out within the general pick areas. Still other warehouses have put system identifiers on the pick documents to alert the pickers. This can be done with a field on the system item master record and tweaking the software to make a notation on the pick document. Either way can help predictability of process but, nonetheless, still requires training and continuous insistence on accuracy of picking and attention to detail. These aids help, but unfortunately are not absolutely foolproof.

Standardized Layering

Another helpful system design aid to support counting accuracy is to maintain standardized layering in the storage areas. For example, a factory in Skelmersdale, England, that manufactures automobile components regularly utilizes standard castings in its process. These castings are brought in from the supplier in standardized plastic egg-carton-type containers, designed to hold exactly twenty-four castings per layer. There are several layers (also standardized) in each container. This type of strategy makes the parts very easy to count accurately. It also keeps the supplier counts accurate. When parts arrive in the receiving area, the pallets can be checked easily and quickly for count accuracy to the packing slip, and when picking components, the same advantage is of help.

Proper Component Protection as Required

Many components have safety issues associated with them that have to be taken into account. This would include flammables, combustibles, and even explosive materials. Obviously, these considerations are important by anybody's standards. It surprising to see how many companies do not design proper methods into their processes.

Additionally, protection of the component itself can be very important. Many parts are subject to rust and corrosion or other deterioration. Some materials can be affected by specifics such as ultraviolet light, heat, moisture, vibration, static electricity, etc. These requirements are always taken into consideration when designing the right storage pattern in high-performance organizations.

Material Handling Equipment

Having the right equipment to access inventory and its availability when needed ensure proper handling and timeliness of material movement. This often means dedicated equipment in areas with high activity. Forklift trucks are not the only consideration. Often pushcarts and/or pallet jack-type equipment is all that is needed. Carousels (discussed later in this chapter) are moving storage racks that move material to the pickers as opposed to equipment that moves the pickers to the material. Carousels can be very effective and eliminate the need for picking vehicles.

Many large distribution facilities traditionally have been overly cost conscious when procuring equipment for their distribution centers. Some-times this can be to the extreme point that the wrong equipment for the process gets into the facility design just because it seems cheaper to buy. Sit-down counter balance trucks are a frequent example. When large SKU (stockkeeping unit) handling is needed for the operation, the driver's visibility can become blocked when driving forward in these vehicles. In most of these operations, out of necessity, the drivers begin to drive backwards when carrying these large loads. While it would seem like an obvious problem, many distribution facilities still utilize these trucks which are unsuited for the application. Two problems result from this forklift misapplication:

1. It can be a safety issue in that excessive back injuries result from drivers operating in a twisted posture for extended periods of time.
2. When drivers operate equipment this way, they tend to have a blind side as they have to look over one shoulder. Many times, they also have to look through side shields that are not always as clear as the frontal lenses in many safety glasses. This has led to pedestrian injuries and other accidents because the drivers did not see the person walking behind them in the warehouse.

Some organizations are starting to look at narrow-aisle equipment in these applications. There can be two advantages:

1. Operators can stand up and drive the truck from both directions. This allows them to drive without being in an uncomfortable or un-safe position.

Narrow-aisle forklift equipment can sometimes be overlooked in warehouse applications. It can have advantages when large loads are common and it is hard to see over the load.

2. The narrow-aisle equipment allows for more dense storage of ma-terial in the same amount of space. This cube utilization can be a cost saver if extra space is needed.

Putting the right equipment in the right area not only makes the job more pleasant and efficient, but also helps ensure timeliness, an important factor in customer service, schedule accountability, and ultimately record accuracy.

Accessible Material

Material should be accessible by authorized personnel. This means inventory is not piled behind something else in an aisle or location. High-performance organizations do not locate inventory in areas that require other inventory to be moved prior to its availability. This inconvenience can discourage proper housekeeping and workplace organization and ultimately accuracy of schedules and data. Everything should have a specific location and be accessible by the people responsible for picking.

At one large manufacturer, distribution was done through large distribution centers scattered throughout North America. Because its product was seasonal, storage requirements changed from month to month. Prior to just a couple of years ago, this organization did not have a formal top-management Sales and Operations Planning (S&OP) process. Each year, the distribution centers would become filled just prior to demand season. In recent years, sales have grown along with market share. Before the S&OP process, there was no communication loop to link demand and buffer inventory decisions to warehouse space requirements. In the spring, the warehouses would fill and eventually there would be no more room available. Given no other alternative, the warehouse people would begin filling the warehouse aisles. This meant that often they would have to move inventory to get to something else required for a pick. The logic everybody in the warehouses used was that after the demand season started, there would be less storage required. No one wanted to request more space because of cost.

When the S&OP process was implemented and management became more aware of decision ramifications, the decision was made quickly to align warehouse space with the decision process. Top management in this company understood that it was not cost effective to store parts more than one deep, making some inventory inaccessible. Costs actually went down as space was managed to planned requirements.

It is useful and helpful, as well as cost effective, to have materials stored in usable space. This rule also assumes, however, that inventory not needed is either not produced or managed out of the process regularly.

Limited Access

There is an old manufacturing saying: "You can't keep inventory away from people who need it to meet their customer's need." Not only is that

> **"You** can't keep inventory from the people who need it for servicing the customer!"

statement probably very popular and familiar, but it also is an interesting thought as we begin to discuss the decision to lock up or not lock up the inventory.

Many companies that have accurate inventories do not lock up the material or limit access through physical barriers. Many managers do not understand this fact and many people actually believe the opposite to be true. What these high-performance organizations do have is an understanding level and an established organizational discipline that ensure a timely transaction for each inventory movement. People must understand the processes and reasons for procedural discipline or they will naturally shortcut the system and corrupt data integrity. In a prior example, a company that used yellow vests was described. In yet another example, a company in the Midwest used hard hats to designate warehouse access. In both cases, people were not locked out nor were they denied access to the inventory.

Psychological barriers such as the yellow vests or the hard hats, if accompanied with proper disciplines, are more effective than fences in the long run. The difference is management expectation, follow-up, and accountability.

Specific and Unique Location Identification

Simply stated, just as every place on earth normally has an address, every place in the plant or warehouse should have a recognizable address for reference. Racks should have separate location addresses for each pallet opening on each level. An exception can be made when the rack is used to accommodate bulk storage for one SKU. In that case, it can be appropriate to have the rack itself labeled as one location. Only one SKU would normally be stored in that rack.

This methodology applies to all of a warehouse. Locations should be sized appropriately. It is better to err on the "too many" location side than the "not enough" side. When a hierarchal location system is used, it can be very easy to change location sizes depending on the need. We will continue to pursue this thought throughout this chapter.

Unfortunately, in old computer systems there often is a barrier to location design choice. In some older computer systems, especially those that have never added a warehouse management module, multiple location capability is not part of the system design. This can leave some warehouse managers wondering where to go next.

In other organizations where backflushing (automatic issue transactions triggered from another system action) is used, the system has restrictions on location identifiers because of overall inventory balancing requirements. In some of these computer systems, again mostly older ones, the business system is not advanced enough to recognize from which location the parts are to be transacted. In these companies, there is little choice except to have everything in one generic location that allows the system to always deduct from the right location. (How could it go wrong?)

In both of these situations, system constraints can force organizations to abandon real location balance management. It is not unheard of to do the unthinkable — have an off-line system. (I have to admit it is hard for me to write this!) In some specific cases, it is acceptable (and, yes, desirable) to have an off-line, spreadsheet-type inventory tracking system until better integrated systems can be installed. This is the case if management is in full support of location balances and also wants to reduce inventory significantly in the process. Reducing inventory usually makes knowing what you have and where it is much more of a requirement. If backflushing is the only issue causing system restraints, alternatives should be explored, including limitations on backflushing. This can be done by segregating the warehouse inventory and only using backflush transactions after inventory has been transacted out of the warehouse balances. More detail will follow.

Adequate Availability of System Tools

Lack of proper access to the system, as was stated with other tools such as material handling equipment, can become a deterrent to high levels of accuracy. High-performance organizations have system access in all areas that require it. This can include scanning equipment, terminals, reports, audit trails, etc. Make it easy for employees to be timely and accurate.

Point-of-Use Storage

Many high-performance organizations are eliminating their main storage areas and opting for storage at point of use (POU). The rules for storage accuracy do not change. Regardless of where the inventory is kept, it has to be neat and organized for proper accuracy disciplines. Transactions must be both understood and executed in a timely manner. Obviously, these same organizations are continuing to eliminate inventory in their systems, and by limiting the storage to just the floor, the warehouse buffers become savings opportunities — provided there are good controls in place. If the result is more shortages, sometimes the savings are difficult to see. Any location balance stored on the line for more than twenty-four hours is considered "controlled" inventory and should be audited and controlled for high levels of accuracy. Training and education become more important as more and more people get their hands in the inventory transaction pie.

In one plant in Anderson, South Carolina, prior to a plant-wide accuracy blitz, the warehouse manager used backflushing from the receiving dock to the finished goods area. It was determined that there were opportunities to reduce inventory levels and cost by improving inventory accuracy. The warehouse manager decided that the "controlled inventory" or inventory that was by plan in place for more than twenty-four hours needed to be segregated from other fast-moving inventory, usually part of work in process. The warehouse locations were easy to determine as needing a "control" factor, but he was also convinced that there were POU storage areas that also needed similar transaction controls. An investigation found that there were, in fact, seventy-five locations in the factory within the production areas where inventory was stored regularly for more than twenty-four hours. They were designated as warehouse locations even though they physically were not in the warehouse. Again, training and support from management were required to change plant behaviors. After all, it made no sense to have warehouse people come out to do the transactions as required on the factory when others were capable with the right knowledge.

Storage Patterns

There are various storage patterns that can be used in storing inventory. These include:

- Dedicated
- Primary
- Random

- Zone
- Golden zone

There are others, and some of these have been called different names, but this covers the main methods. Each has its place in manufacturing and each has advantages and disadvantages. It is helpful to understand the differences so that the right method can be used in your application.

Dedicated Storage or Primary Location Storage

Inventory that is stored in the same place or places each time it is received is called dedicated or primary location storage. In a grocery store, typically the milk is always stored in the same location. Dedicated storage methodology employs the same type of behavior. "A place for everything and everything in its place." While this seems logical and applicable in all cases, it is not always the best answer. There are both pluses and minuses.

Advantages

Employees always know where to look for certain inventory. Sometimes, as in the case of silos for powder or resins, there is little choice but to have dedicated storage. Not to continue the same material in the same silo would cause contamination issues that could be very costly and could cause quality problems in the process.

In some cases, odd-shaped or large items require special handling and storage requirements that play well into a primary location methodology.

Disadvantages

Primary locations or dedicated storage systems are by design rather inflexible. When schedules are increased or decreased on certain products, storage space changes. If parts become obsolete or if new parts are often added, space can be wasted and/or inadequate. Lack of flexibility can be a problem.

Application

Most POU storage is an application for dedicated or primary location storage patterns. As stated, with big, odd-shaped, or especially high-volume components, dedicated storage can be a plus. Examples could include methods such as silo storage, refrigeration, hazardous waste storage, large items, items with shelf life, highly valuable items with special control needs, etc. Companies that have high volumes sometimes use regulation of delivery schedules as the offset to required storage capacity restraints. Just in time (JIT) and vendor-managed inventory are both helpful in keeping this regulation in place. This negates the problem of physical location capacity tied to the schedule.

When primary locations are assigned, it is almost always a mistake to arrange items (SKUs) in numerical or alphabetical order. You will spend most of your time rearranging the warehouse every time a change is introduced.

Note: When primary locations are used for the main storage methodology, it is almost always a mistake to organize locations in numerical or alphabetical order. Doing this takes away any flexibility that exists with this already limited process. When new items are added, the entire warehouse must be reorganized to accommodate the addition. Not good!

Random Storage

In a random location storage system, inventory is always put away in the first available slot as it arrives. Inventory from different shipments generally is not consolidated with prior stock unless there are capacity issues requiring this practice. As a rule, all receipts go into empty locations. This is a favored methodology with many seasoned warehouse veterans. It has some good advantages in the right application.

Random locations systems are favored by most seasoned warehouse experts. They offer the most benefits, including flexibility.

Advantages

There are several advantages to random storage. The following list represents some of the more important advantages.

1. Empty locations are always utilized. This is not true in a primary system. Some locations can be empty, but because they are not

designated for incoming product, they are not used without creating an exception process.

2. There is no restriction on how much or how little material is stored. The locations always match the need because as inventory is brought in, it is put away in whatever locations are available. This continues to be a plus as long as the warehouse itself is not capacity restricted.

3. Each time a location is emptied, it is zeroed out, allowing for stock balance checks at zero quantity. There is no easier or faster time to cycle count inventory than when the inventory balance is at zero. In many applications, an "empty verification" card/ticket is attached to the location each time a new skid of components is put away. When the material handler or stock picker empties the last part, he or she pulls the ticket and hands it to the dispatcher. The dispatcher then uses the ticket to verify a zero balance, which also places the location automatically on the "empties" list. While this does not take the place of good inventory control or substitute for robust cycle counting procedures, it is a good cleansing process for the location balances and the methodology adds almost no cost. It is for these reasons that random location is a preferred methodology in many warehouses and is highly recommended by this author in the right applications.

> The easiest time to cycle count a location is when it is at "zero balance." Random locations not only allow this to be done easily, but are designed to promote this process behavior.

Disadvantages

Random location storage, when used regularly, requires locator capability in the business system. This system methodology also can require more space unless inventory is controlled in small quantity flows (JIT principles are utilized). This space inefficiency arises simply because all locations are emptied as the material is used up before new inventory is put into the location. At any one time, there can be several low-quantity balances in storage as replenishment cycles through the process. This can result in several locations with the same inventory in them, one with little inventory and one with the new receipt. If location management is sized correctly and there are enough smaller locations to accommodate today's more frequent deliveries, this disadvantage can be minimized.

Application

Most general warehouses can use a random location storage system effectively. Random location storage is generally accepted as the method of choice in high-performance inventory control associated with central storage. It does not have to be used exclusively in any facility as it is often mixed with other methodologies such as zone storage, described next.

In Syracuse, New York, a distribution center for material handling manufacturing components has well over 24,000 separate locations and maintains a 95+ percent accuracy by location by utilizing random location storage. This warehouse incorporates carousels as well as rack order picking and finds the random location methodology to be most suitable to low cost and high predictability of accuracy. This is especially important in its distribution of aftermarket service parts worldwide. Its customers demand high service and the warehouse provides it.

Zone Storage

In a zone storage methodology, inventory is randomly stored in location "zones." This is done to make the picking of some materials more efficient and/or, in other cases, certain types of inventory need to be in a specific area because of characteristics. For example, frozen food in a grocery warehouse is only stored in the freezer. In that case, the freezer locations would be considered a zone. In another example, a warehouse that stores steel, might store flat plate in an area configured differently than where bar stock would be stored. In both cases, the material could be stored randomly within specifically designated zones. There are numerous examples one could come up with to suggest applications.

It is possible to use dedicated or primary location methods within zone storage. It may even be necessary given certain shapes and sizes of inventory within the zone. It is not recommended, however, when parts are random sizes and shapes within the zone requirement.

Advantages

Picking can be more efficient as parts common to one assembly may be in the same area. In a tractor weld area of one factory, for example, the parts for the tractor weldment were all stored in the same area, making the picking extremely efficient. The picker could simply walk down the aisle and pick all the parts for the weldment without requiring much travel or extra movement.

Also, in zone storage, location patterns match the size, shape, and special needs of specific parts. The advantages are similar to primary location systems. When incorporated with random location designs, within the zones, sometimes the best of all worlds can be enjoyed.

Disadvantages

In many applications, zone storage methodology is used as an answer to restrictive needs such as refrigeration, explosive-proof cabinetry, perishable material storage, etc., with special storage requirements that are not suited or cost effective for the entire warehouse. In reality, there are few disadvantages to zone storage methodology when done correctly with random locations.

Flexibility is, however, a consideration with the use of zone storage. As production plans fluctuate, these specific zones need to also expand and contract or the result can be forced process deviation and additional cost. Often the process efficiency advantages of zone storage make it worth the risks.

Application

There are an almost infinite number of applications for zone storage. Some of these include:

- Electronics components that require special handling such as a static-free environment
- High-value items such as diamond chips used in aggregate manufacturing
- Groceries requiring humidity or refrigeration
- Retail sales such is in grocery stores
- Numerous other high-volume picking operations

Golden Zoning

Golden zoning is a specific variation of the zone storage discussed above. Golden zoning can offer the best answer in many applications. Like zone storage, golden zoning limits the areas in which specific items can be stored randomly. The biggest difference is generated from the management of locations within the established zones.

Typically, the first step to set up golden zoning is to gather pertinent data. It is important to both understand and acknowledge the frequency of pick requirements for each component within already-established zones. Remember that the golden zoning is a subgroup of zoning, so the item groups would already be established based on commonalities of storage requirements, shared consumption, or other reasons for segregation.

The most ergonomically friendly locations and the locations easiest and most efficiently picked are where the most frequent picks are to be concentrated. This requires observation of pick habits and analysis of volume requirements, not only historically but also planned in the future. For example, in grocery wholesale warehouse application, canned vegetables typically are stored in a common area defined within the larger warehouse. In this application, the "fast movers" (items that have frequent demand) are stored at the most accessible locations within the canned vegetable zone. This allows the least amount of forklift travel both horizontally and vertically and supports efficiency of picking operations.

It may be of interest that golden zoning is also the storage method used in retail stores as well. Other drivers determine the positioning, however. For example, candy is placed within children's reach, vegetables and fruit are the first products encountered because of margins, and milk is often in the back of the store to get consumers to walk through other areas.

In assembly operations, it often makes sense to have assembly components stored in the same area that they will be consumed for pick efficiency. This would apply to all assembly requirements such as gluing, soldering, welding, and/or fastener assembly. By locating the parts both in the right vicinity of the consuming operation and in the easiest locations within the zone for picker access, all advantages are gained.

Carousel storage, storage equipment that brings the parts to the pickers, is very efficient in the right application. Available in both vertical and horizontal applications, carousels in themselves are zones effected by the size and volume of the parts stored. Within the carousel, one might put high moving parts in the storage bins located from chest high to just below the waist. This minimizes the amount of stooping and bending as well as stretching upward, thus minimizing costly and otherwise harmful injuries. In one application in Greene, New York, a manufacturer has lift mechanisms that lift pickers up and down vertically to increase the golden zone of picking in its carousel application. (Carousels will be discussed in detail later in this chapter.)

Advantages

Golden zoning shares all of the advantages of random storage with the addition of more efficient picking. Because ergonomics can often come into play in the planning of golden zones, there can also be benefits not only in efficiency but also in employee and equipment efficiencies. By carefully planning golden zones in distribution facilities or manufacturing, additional gains can be made in both safety and maintenance due to reduced wear and tear on humans and equipment alike.

Disadvantages

Industry today has to be flexible to maintain a competitive advantage. Flexibility means changing requirements. When utilizing golden zoning, most likely plans can and will fluctuate, especially in flexible environments. When this happens, the data driving the establishment of the golden zones can change. The need for the golden zone to expand or contract or to totally change can result. Even with this fact, proper planning can minimize the risks of flexibility. Golden zoning is often the right answer in many distribution and warehouse applications. Golden zoning as a storage design opportunity should be in your tool kit.

Application

It should be no surprise that many of the zone storage applications are shared with golden zoning. Applications include grocery, retail sales, high-volume picking operations, carousel storage, POU storage, and/or work cell storage. Golden zoning applies to any storage environment where people are picking parts with different usage rates or travel requirements. It minimizes travel and/or cycle time to pick components and reduces strains and injuries.

Storage Layout

Several methods of storing material have been described to this point. These methods support various processes within the order fulfillment stage of a manufacturing or service organization. In deciding where to store material, there are a few reminders:

1. During normal pick operations, does the material storage area force or require backtracking in the process flow? It goes without saying

that this should be minimized. Often storage layout can affect this efficiency.

2. Are there limiting factors such as availability of material handling equipment? Overhead cranes, floor scales, and other devices are sometimes critical in the flow and need to be considered. Sharing equipment can be common and is often not considered in the storage design.

3. Business plan considerations such as forecasted growth and product line fluctuations play a part in the design of material storage. Most manufacturing organizations today are introducing new equipment at intervals never seen before. Storage considerations need to be flexible in today's environment.

4. Safety is one of the most important considerations in any warehouse or factory design. Some components (such as flammables or explosives) have regulations requiring certain storage containers or methods of handling. Many of the safety concerns have government regulation tied to them and need to be considered.

> **S**afety is a very high priority in high-performance organizations today for many reasons. The warehouse is no exception.

5. Accessibility for the users is an important consideration. It is most efficient to have material readily available. This would be a consideration in POU storage and is a factor in golden zoning. On the more obvious but still misapplied front, items need to be at the location face. In too many warehouses, poor practices and storage design allow items to become inaccessible because some are piled in front of others. Access can only happen after first moving other items. This is very bad!

Carousels for Storage

Carousels, moving racks that store components and finished parts for specific order picking, are hidden gems in the storage equipment world. Carousels are not as common as perhaps they should be. While they are not the answer in every application, they may just deserve a second look. In a carousel application, the storage locations move to the picker rather than the picker going to the storage locations. This can affect pick efficiency by utilizing the travel time normally wasted by moving humans and having only the inventory move. If the operator uses this time productively with processes such as packaging or kitting the components, the total time required for a group of part picks can be reduced dramatically.

A widely recognized application with which you immediately may be familiar is the dry-cleaning business. Carousel racking often is used to bring a customer's garment to the front of the store. When tied to a location system, this can save the storekeeper time in finding the garment.

Industrial carousels used in manufacturing work much the same as those in the local cleaners; they are just bigger and more robust. Industrial carousels have been in existence for years. In Europe, they have been popular in many applications. In the U.S., initially they were used most widely in distribution applications such as wholesale consumer goods.

In the early 1980s, carousels received renewed positive press through marketing efforts by carousel manufacturers. Today, they are utilized in many more nondistribution applications such as manufacturing, although they have never really captured the interest of mainstream warehouse professionals for some reason. Most manufacturing managers do not consider them at all. My experience suggests that renewed enthusiasm for carousels in the right applications should be given a second look.

Industrial carousels can offer an easy method for quick access to inventory from hard demand, especially with today's software capabilities and technology that make possible linkages to an organization's order signals. If a company is involved with customer order picking or kitting of small materials or components, and has not yet improved processes to the point of eliminating buffer inventory, carousel storage can be helpful and offer efficient picking capability. Many retail distribution operations (TV shopping networks, Internet sales distribution, sporting goods mail-order businesses, etc.) have found carousels to be effective. The ease of access, worker efficiency in picks per hour, and space utilization advantages make this an idea worth pursuing in certain applications.

If you are wondering how carousels work, they are simple in design. When hooked to order management and proper software, the orders are batched and pick signals are sent to the carousel computer controller from the inventory control system. In retail order picking (and other applications), often two or three carousels are positioned with one pick station. As one component item is picked from one of these clustered carousels, another carousel is rotating the next pick requirement to position in front of the picker/pick station. Conveyor systems can consolidate multiple pick stations for single-order requirements, where they can be boxed and shipped or sent to the line for assembly. When there is no travel time spent in the process, one can imagine the efficiency improvements enjoyed over standard order-picking truck applications.

One forklift manufacturer has most of its aftermarket service distribution requirements stored in carousels. In its main distribution facility, these carousels are double stacked (two carousels high). To make picks possible, pick platforms are utilized for the second tier of carousels. This eliminates the need for material handling equipment and the transporting of pickers throughout the warehouse — which is interesting given the fact that this company is a world leader in the manufacturing of forklift equipment including order-picking vehicles!

Location Systems

The location label or identifier is the indicator that resides in the inventory management or warehouse system that tells the storekeeper or stock picker where to find the item needed. Location labels normally do not change frequently. Given this fact, location labels are most convenient if the fields or characters that make up the label are "intelligent." Reading from left to right, each additional digit or alpha character in the location should give another clue as to the whereabouts of the needed item. A U.S. zip code is an example of a location label. Each digit gets the user closer to the detailed location. Location labels within a distribution or manufacturing facility work the same way.

> The U.S. zip code system is an example of a hierarchal location system. These work very well and are flexible in design.

All racks and bins areas in the entire facility should be clearly labeled and readable from twenty-five feet away. This means both inside the warehouse as well as POU locations within the manufacturing areas. High-performance organizations will have these location signs professionally painted in block letters at least six inches in height and hang them at the ends of each rack. One organization that uses man-up order-picker-type forklift vehicles equipped with spotlights uses reflective labels for the location markers on the racks so they will not be missed or misread. This makes the labels light up and much easier to read, which can eliminate some careless pick errors. An example of a location label including the progression of information is provided in Figure 7-3.

Time and consideration are worth the effort when developing a new location identifier system. The objective is to make the location system

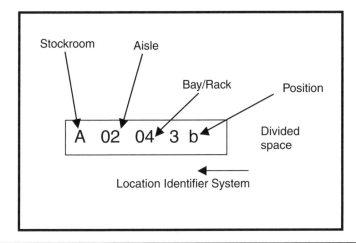

Figure 7-3. Sample location label.

easy to see and to understand. It should also be consistent throughout the facility. The payback is in training costs saved and improved accuracy. Some rules to remember:

- Easy-to-use and easy-to-understand location system, combined with
- A well-organized storage area, with
- Locations properly fitted to the product stored

This sets the stage for accurate inventory records. Many organizations grid the entire facility and include this grid pattern on both maps and blueprints of the facility and on all location labels. The grid becomes part of the location hierarchy, as shown in Figure 7-3. Good, sound location systems can be used for years, as they can grow with the business. Next we will talk about training, possibly one of the most important elements of process control.

8

Day 15 and Beyond: Training for Process Control

Day 15

On day 15, activity should be well developed. Begin documentation of the procedures as soon as processes are determined, even before day 15. Some procedures should already be confirmed by day 15, thus allowing training to start.

Introduction

Successful training is usually the difference between excessive variability and consistency in the inventory control process. Of course, that statement assumes the process design is appropriate. Training, like education, is non-negotiable in the pursuit of data accuracy. In most organizations attacking data accuracy, there is a need to change not only procedures but also the culture within the walls of the business. Training is one of the best ways to affect culture quickly.

Education and training are the best and quickest levers to affect company culture.

Employees should be trained on different topics depending on their duties and responsibilities. This includes cycle counting, transaction dis-

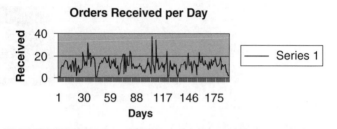

Figure 8-1. Most businesses receive varied order levels day to day.

cipline, and different work areas such as receiving, put-away, or delivery. Flexibility obviously increases as employees are cross-trained and can be involved in other responsibilities as work fluctuates with customer demand shifts. Orders are hardly ever consistent day to day (Figure 8-1). Customers in almost every market are somewhat unruly. Well-designed training can create an awareness of this flexibility expectation if it is a component of each training session.

When focusing on data accuracy, there are often specific transactions required for certain job functions. People working in a production or distribution warehouse, for example, probably need to know much more about inventory transactions than the maintenance department does. Maintenance people may not be involved actively with production inventory. The maintenance people could even have a separate storage area for machine breakdown and preventative maintenance "wearable"-type components. Although accuracy in maintenance components is just as important as it is in production parts, the transactions often have specific actions associated with the environment. This should be minimized, but is often a reality. These idiosyncrasies in process require specific training for each area. If the transaction procedures are kept similar, the training becomes easier and there is less likelihood of error.

All transactions do not hit the general ledger with the same meaning and impact, and for that same reason, there may be a need to use different transaction codes for maintenance or consumable-type items than for production, inventory-type items. The cost of maintenance items is frequently included as part of the cost of the overhead of an operation. Most production inventory is logged by accounting as an asset on the books. Both inventory categories, however, can benefit from perpetual balances maintained on the computer business system. This is an example where a company can capitalize on the advantages of similarity in process.

It should be easily recognized that, regardless of how the items consumption is logged in the general ledger, accuracy has its benefits. As to the topic of data accuracy, once the documentation is started and at least partially complete, the first step in training is to develop the training plan. Day 15 and this chapter are about training from the documentation, and that is exactly where we are headed.

The Training Plan

A successful training plan starts with developing an understanding of what skill sets are required to support the business objectives. Examples of objectives that might typically be included as priorities are:

- Growth
- Cost improvements
- Changes in product or technology offerings
- Operations excellence

The process of analyzing the gap between existing skills and required skills is referred to as a skills assessment. Data accuracy certainly fits into appropriate business priorities and requires certain skills to maintain. It could be argued that data accuracy would contribute significantly to any or all of the priorities listed above. Doing a skills assessment for a robust inventory accuracy process is much the same exercise and should have similar focus.

Skills required in the new process may also be different than skills required prior to the new focus. For example, yesterday, the expediting or negotiation skills to get suppliers to send items in early and unplanned may have been valued. Today, the new process may value system knowledge and discipline with the same importance. Sometimes people who were successful under the old ways have difficulty under the new rules. Training can narrow this gap.

Start by listing the activities or processes that are identified as changing. This might include simple skills like using scanners or more complex skills like following transaction audit trails in the business system. Continue to develop this list by documenting any skills or knowledge that will be required under the new process. This exercise becomes the list of existing

Education is the "why." Training is the "how." Both are critical in high-performance organizations. They must be part of the plan.

skills that will be defined as the "is" condition which can then be compared to the required skills defined as the "should be" condition.

Once this skills assessment is complete, plans for implementation of the training can be developed. Both education and training are required to build the bridge between the "is" and "should be" conditions. In Chapter 3, the case was made that educating personnel early in the data accuracy implementation process was key to having "buy in" to the need for the basic disciplines involved with data integrity. Education, which is different than training, was the energy required in the "buy in" phase, very early in the data accuracy focus. At day 15 and beyond, while education will continue in some capacity forever, we now introduce the need for training.

The word "training," as used in this text, refers to the transfer of process and procedural knowledge to those in the organization who need it. Education deals heavily with the "why" we need to do this new procedure, whereas training is more the "how" it will be executed.

What Up-Front Training Is Required?

Training for inventory accuracy starts with having the team members achieve an understanding of the basics of required transactions and how these transactions impact both the inventory and the business. In-house experts who are well versed in inventory transaction procedures usually deliver this training. Great care and thought should be administered when determining the teaching resource to lead this education. True empowerment requires people who have excellent understanding of the processes. By making sure the delivery is appropriate, the results can be more predictably positive. Sometimes this means that management may have to take an active role to coach the right resource into this important training position during the launch of process changes.

During this first training step, the objective is to list the needs of each area and what exact training needs each will require. This training list would include specific types of transactions and how to do them using the correct computer system screens. Using a process map of the required steps can be extremely helpful and will minimize overlooking some of the specifics.

Table 8-1 is an example of a logical list of activities that need clarification delivered through training. This list is not intended to represent a complete chart of departments and needs. A chart similar to this example should be customized for each application within the organization.

Table 8-1. Inventory Training Needs

Department	Inventory Accuracy Training Needs
Warehouse	Receiving, Issuing Put-Away Miscellaneous Issues Miscellaneous Receipts Adjustments Cycle Counting Rejects and Scrap
Assembly	Returns Rejects Scrap Point-of-Use Storage Transactions Closing of Work Orders
Fabrication	Raw Material Transactions Rejects Scrap
Materials/Office	Miscellaneous Issues Miscellaneous Receipts Closing of Work Orders

Who Needs the Training?

All warehouse personnel, factory supervisors, and team leaders should be included in the data accuracy procedural training. Additionally, production personnel need to be involved if there are transactions that need to be done by them. In some environments, team leaders perform all of the scrap transactions. This is not such a bad idea as it keeps an eye on the scrap produced and allows for proper root cause analysis to be done in a timely fashion.

Each training session should be tailored to the areas, duties, and people in the class. A training matrix works well to capture and account for all training and qualifications needed for accurately executing transactions (see Table 8-2).

As they are hired, new employees need special training attention. These newcomers, depending on their background, often do not have the same level of understanding and appreciation for accuracy as the rest of the newly trained department personnel. For the sake of maintaining record

Table 8-2.   Training Matrix

Name	Transaction				
	4	5	6	7	8
Joe Smith	Q	Q	Q	Q	Q
Jane Doe	Q	Q	Q	Q	Q
Jack Rand		T	T	T	
Sally Brown	T	T			

Q = qualified, T = scheduled for training.

accuracy and to minimize periodic dips in the accuracy level, the potential gap created by employee turnover should be addressed.

This is important enough to digress for just a bit. Along with procedural training, the education already given to the existing employees is also important for new resources. The initial education discussed in Chapter 3 typically would be incorporated into an ongoing training package. An appropriate orientation process should include an enterprise resource planning (ERP) overview as well as education on the importance of inventory accuracy and transaction disciplines as a component of ERP performance.

New employees have to be given the same training or process degradation will occur over time. Plan it as part of the initial process and it will not be overlooked.

At Grafco PET Packaging, a leader in PET plastics packaging products, a regular training package is available and delivered to all new employees. It includes an introduction to their continuous improvement process. Employees are introduced to the management system elements of accountability as well as metrics and importance of data accuracy in the fiber of the Grafco culture. It has proven to be very successful.

What Resources Are Needed to Deliver the Training?

The training sessions should be led by people who have to enforce the execution disciplines in the area. This is typically the supervisors, first-line management, or the inventory task team members responsible for plant-wide accuracy. It has been proven in many applications that the best people to enforce behavior in the area are the same persons to whom people report. Departmental outsiders can struggle with clout if the first-line managers or supervisors are not engaged. Using them for delivery of training puts them in the position of having to know the procedures and committing to walk the talk.

When Can the Resources Be Available for the Required Sessions?

Capacity planning may seem pretty obvious, but is often not planned into the training process. It is a necessary part of any project or process implementation including data accuracy. The training schedule would include the availability of resources if it is to be successful. Higher management is sometimes needed to step in and enforce priorities in environments where there never seems to be time to do this important training. Backups for all training resources should be identified early in the process design to keep the factory going during peak demand. These backups can also become a second tier of instructors for training of new hires as well.

When Can the Attendees Be Available?

Doing training or education after hours is a mistake in most environments. The employees are looking for signals as to the priority of this effort. When management is willing to provide the time during production hours for ongoing training and education, the message is strong that this is a management priority. The opposite is true when training is done off-hours, even when overtime pay is given. If training is part of the fiber of the organization, it needs to be scheduled just as preventative maintenance would be done. Training should be done during normal business hours if at all possible. Backups/substitutes should be scheduled and provided in those areas where coverage is critical.

> **E**ducation and training delivered on employee "overtime" gives employees the impression that this is not "how we run the business." Instead it has the flavor of a special one-time event.

This "during work hours" rule should not be confused with employee-driven education such as continuing education or APICS (American Production and Inventory Control Society) education that may be done during evenings in preparation for degrees or APICS certification. These types of sessions are well suited for evenings.

One Massachusetts plastics company that emphasizes this point shuts down operations an entire day every month to do ongoing education and training for factory personnel. The president of that company believes in education as one of the most important investments. He says it is the company's investment in human capital. By shutting down the whole operations department, the organization is able to schedule training easily without conflict. It also sends a powerful signal to the organization about the importance of human resources and thought leadership within this company.

A clothing manufacturer in Pennsylvania uses education as a reward for completing the season successfully. In this particular market, the majority of this seasonal product ships by early summer. This allows for a summer retreat sponsored by the company. Each time, an outside resource is engaged to deliver education on some topic. While this is not always on the topic of inventory accuracy, the message here is one that has great application in numerous companies including yours.

The bottom line — make sure the employees are available for the training. Help them when it seems impossible to break away. Often only management can make that happen.

What Course and/or Instructor Materials Are Required?

By providing students and instructors with written materials, either in hard copy or on a computer or television screen, students have the opportunity to learn more easily. The use of more than one sensory skill (in this case, hearing and sight) increases the learning efficiency. There are video products available today that have companion student workbooks and instructor manuals. I have actually been involved in developing such projects. APICS also has materials available that are designed for novice delivery and in most cases are quite thorough.

It is generally understood that students retain only 25 to 50 percent of what they hear even in the short term. With the advantage of seeing the material discussed, that learning efficiency increases to 50 to 75 percent short term. (We will not even discuss the efficiency when longer term retention is added to the equation!) When people can interact with the materials, learning and retention increase greatly. This makes a case for using a teaching style or product that utilizes some type of interaction between the instructor and the student.

It should be noted that purchased materials never completely take the place of facility-specific training materials. The best training packages and

The best teaching designs take into consideration the company's actual documentation. Exercises can be developed around them, leading employees to have a deeper understanding of the need for disciplines behind them.

materials guide instructors to incorporate their own procedure documents into the training. It is also helpful to have exercises incorporated into the training that take specific facility opportunities into consideration. When people help find the answers, they are always more eager to implement them. The best "canned" training program packages and products design exercises into the offerings to facilitate discussions using the company's own procedural documents.

Are Facilities Available In-House or Do You Need to Arrange Outside Facilities?

Surroundings make a great deal of difference when trying to optimize training time and effectiveness. In high-performance organizations, training facilities are located on company grounds. Some plants have very elaborate soundproof rooms designed for efficient learning with Internet access, video equipment, overhead projection equipment, and flip charts for note-taking and problem-solving activities. Companies that are serious about human capital plan for success by providing high-quality facilities to deliver their investment in this human capital. This investment in human capital is training and education.

A plastics company in Baltimore recently remodeled the offices at its biggest facility. The center of this remodeling was a training room with state-of-the-art technologies allowing video linkage to all facilities at once. In this company, communication and training are essential to the successful continuance of competitive advantage. Top management is committed to the point that it is leading the charge. Management's actions and expectations clearly support the company's continuous improvement process element of its culture.

What Is the Best Way to Deliver Quality Training and Maintain Consistency?

Training should be delivered consistently throughout all shifts and by all instructors. This can best be accomplished through train-the-trainer education for all instructors and by standardizing training documents such as procedures, policies, and application examples incorporating the business system software. Many organizations have these materials loaded to a shared drive on the server for easy access facility-wide. Remember, though, that along with this access, training for accessibility as well as investments in proper equipment are necessary to get the biggest benefit from the investment.

As a preface to the procedural training, an educational overview often reminds employees of the need for this new discipline and supports better buy in of the new procedures. Video-based inventory accuracy training segments can help deliver this education element while adding an alternative delivery medium to increase material retention and consistency. These products are available on the market at various prices and quality levels. My experience with some of these has been excellent. They are worth a look.

Video education products are usually available on DVD and can be loaded to the server for shared access. The best ones support student interaction created with workbook exercises. Prices can be in the four figures, but with the payback and cost to develop them internally, this can actually be a bargain — if they are used properly. "Used properly" means disciplined, scheduled times with mandatory participation. Management participates and discussion is encouraged by all. Actions should result from the discussions, making each session very productive for the business.

The best people to deliver training in their departments are the managers. The old saying is true: "To teach is to learn twice."

The best people to deliver training in their departments are the managers. The old saying is true: "To teach is to learn twice."

Measure the Results

The most obvious way to confirm that the training has been successful is through measured improvement — results in inventory accuracy improvement. Since real company-wide accuracy often takes a few weeks after the training classes, two ways to verify success more quickly are:

1. Have a verbal discussion to indicate understanding at the end of each session. Encourage participation and document decisions, assignments, and actions on a flip chart.
2. Use a quiz to test understanding.

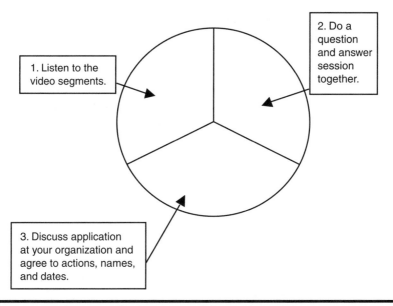

1. Listen to the video segments.

2. Do a question and answer session together.

3. Discuss application at your organization and agree to actions, names, and dates.

Figure 8-2.   The most effective way to deliver video training.

Since video-based inventory accuracy education is often a part of the training as described in this chapter and in Chapter 3, it is worth mentioning here that there is a right and wrong method to deliver video-based education. Never give a video lesson to people with the intention of them taking it home to watch — even in a (missed) class makeup situation. The material is rarely retained this way. Realistically, putting employees in a dark room with a technical training or educational DVD with no facilitation is a good way to provide a paid afternoon nap for the participants.

The most effective video delivery involves a three-step process for increased effectiveness (Figure 8-2):

1. Watch the video lesson. At the end of the video, ask questions about the material. Get attendees to provide some interpretation of the material presented.
2. Discuss prepared questions. The best video educational tools provide both workbooks and instructor's guides.
3. Determine the action items or steps that would apply these new ideas to the company environment. A flip chart or white board should be used to document actions and agreements. The action

items agreed upon should be distributed to participants and followed up on in future sessions.

Institutionalize the Training Process

The quality and consistency of materials are key elements of successful
training. If well-written procedures and training outlines as well as repu-
table sources (for outside educational materials) are utilized, the class
materials can be packaged and used over and over again with new employees and those changing job functions. Good materials also allow and even
promote the use of an expanding group of qualified trainers.

Documentation Prior to Training

In Chapters 4, 5, and 6, discussion centered on understanding the process
flow, understanding the effects of transactions, and creating consistency in
practice through documentation of standard operating procedures.

Key employees are involved with these efforts to create the right process
decisions. Some of them include cycle counters, warehouse team leaders
and managers, line supervisors, material handlers, etc. These key employees are the factory resources that will lead others in finding opportunities
for process control and accuracy improvement. Knowing this, it is worth
making sure these are the first people to get educated in the principles of
high-performance data management. Along with the implementation of
key performance metrics, their education will allow them to begin meaningful process control design work. They can then apply the techniques
and begin to document their solutions. These are also the people to
incorporate in the initial accuracy task team.

There is no reason to believe the training should wait until all the
documentation is complete. Education and training are an ongoing effort
that is scheduled week after week, month after month, year after year in
high-performance companies. If it has not been started, it should be now!
People responsible for the documentation should have as much knowledge
as possible as they go about writing practices and procedures. In many
cases, as soon as a procedure is finished, training can begin. Training in
process-mapping and problem-solving elements is a great consideration.

9

Day 45: Cycle Counting and Auditing Process Control

Day 45
By day 45, the process will have been defined, the documen-
tation well on its way toward completion, and the control
group methodology will have identified root causes with cor-
rective actions. Cycle counting is the next step.

Introduction

Cycle counting is the process of randomly sampling the inventory location balances in a planned method. This means that while checks are done at random, there is a planning element that makes sure certain parts are "randomly" selected within certain time periods, usually monthly, quarterly, or yearly buckets.

Many organizations stratify their inventory by value. Called ABC stratification, this layering can be designed to be and is useful for cycle counting and other inventory control purposes. Using ABC stratification, the inventory is layered into categories by value, criticality, and worth to the organization. Parts are counted at planned intervals depending on this assigned value. ABC inventory stratification is covered in detail later in this chapter.

Although it is probably the most popular method in high-performance businesses, the process of systematically counting existing inventory does not necessarily have to utilize ABC stratification. Other commonly executed methods of cycle counting involve planned counts of racks or areas within the storage areas. In this approach, inventory counts are planned by area rather than value. Either way is acceptable, but they can differ in cost to implement depending on availability of software tools and layout of inventory locations. Cycle counting is the process of planned periodic checking for process control of location balance accuracy. It could be thought of much like an inspection process that is normally considered a cost-added activity. From my experience, unfortunately, it is a necessary evil in the beginning stages of inventory integrity. Few companies eliminate the need for cycle counting.

> **C**ycle counting is the process of planned periodic checking for process control of location balance accuracy.

Some organizations start cycle counting before they have proper controls in place. By numerous counts, they are able to find and repair balances. This is a misuse of cycle counting to "fix" inaccurate balances. This approach alone does not result in process control and can add unnecessary cost to the operation. Cycle counting often correctly utilizes the best warehouse people and takes them away from other value-added activities. Remember that cycle counting is not the goal. Cycle counting is just a required step on the way to world-class data management.

> **R**emember that cycle counting is not the goal. Cycle counting is just a required step on the way to world-class data management.

Physical Inventory

I enjoy talking about physical wall-to-wall inventory activity. It is one of the most frequent activities with absolutely no value to the organization. Many manufacturing, distribution, and processing facilities still do periodic physical inventories. A "physical inventory," as it is usually called, is a count and reconciliation of all materials within the facility, wall to wall, at one designated time. Often, production is completely or partially shut down for this event. Some organizations even take two or more days to count the inventory and then reconcile for weeks or months. This is, without question, a cost-added activity. The wages paid to employees as they count, as well as lost production and capacity, are large costs to pay — especially given the fact that process variation in the form of inaccurate counts is unavoidable in a wall-to-wall physical. Typically, the counters used for these efforts are not accustomed to counting for eight hours a day, and some just do not have the same level of quality concerns as do the company's auditors who often observe the event. There might even be a few counters whose only goal and main motivation are to "finish as soon as possible." Perhaps this idea has a familiar ring to you.

One misnomer is also associated with the metric for successful inventory control. Auditors are mainly concerned with monetary accuracy. It is not that they do not care about piece-part count accuracy; they just do not use that information by itself. This allows mistakes in inventory shrinkage (when the physical count converted to monetary value is less than the current dollar amount record on the accounting books) to offset counts for other part counts that are inaccurate on the high side. This was discussed earlier in this book, but is worth restating.

Some organizations have been known to claim high accuracy based on minimal inventory shrink. The truth is scary. Little about process control is really known from the inventory shrinkage value alone. Actual part counts counted as hits or misses, not converted to currency, tell a much more complete story.

Table 9-1 shows some of the reasons why a physical wall-to-wall inventory is not an acceptable substitute for cycle counting. Let's look at these topics individually:

Table 9-1. Results of Physical Versus Cycle Counting

Goal	Cycle Counting	Periodic Physical
Timely understanding of root cause	Yes	No
Reduction of SKU identifier errors	Yes	No
Minimum loss of production	Yes	No
Helps to sustain overall inventory accuracy	Yes	No
Helps reduce obsolete/excessive inventory	Yes	No
Allows valid materials planning	Yes	No
Supports accurate statement of assets	Yes	Not sure

- **Timely detection of errors** — Cycle counting item locations on a regular basis identifies errors much quicker than only doing a yearly physical count. Errors happen, even in the best environments — remember that every process has variation. When no checks are made, not only do you leave variation to accumulate, you also do not have a good way of understanding accuracy. Problems can get out of hand and have substantial financial impact before you have the opportunity to know it and do something about it.

> Cycle counting should be done by your best people in the warehouse, not the ones you can most afford to let do it.

- **Reduction of item ID errors** — Cycle counting typically is done by trained personnel. Since wall-to-wall counts often involve other nonwarehouse people, annual physical counts can contribute to errors in balances. Again, if cycle count checks are done periodically, errors caused by normal put-away cycles can be detected prior to major financial impact. This only works if the variation rate is reasonably low due to good process controls.

- **Minimum loss of production time** — The yearly physical usually requires some stoppage of production. Businesses only make money if the production machine is working when it is needed. Extra capacity, planned to allow for a wall-to-wall inventory shutdown, requires expensive machinery to be idled and stock to be manufactured and inventoried prior to the physical inventory. Cycle counting is scheduled regularly, often at shift changes or open shifts (to meet cutoff requirements) without affecting production schedules. No extra inventory is required, and no shutdown is necessary.

- **Sustains overall inventory accuracy** — When errors are found during the physical inventory, it is difficult to understand causes. There is a massive amount of information to deal with in a short time period after a wall-to-wall physical. The chances of root cause detection are much higher when some items are counted more frequently. Also, if location balances are checked every time the buffer cycles to zero inventory, little time is required to count and a cleansing effect is created. Physical inventories are not designed to help in this way.

- **Reduce obsolete/excessive inventory** — Because errors can go undetected for a whole year between balance checks when using annual physical inventory checks, replenishment signals on inaccurate balances are also inaccurate. Balances that are in error to the low side (balance shows less than there really is in a location) can cause a premature replenishment signal and result in excessive inventory. High inventory levels naturally increase exposure to obsolescence. Cycle counting reduces this risk by more frequent checks and more accurate inventory balances overall.

■ **Allows and supports a valid material requirements planning (MRP) plan** — Again, if balances are maintained regularly throughout the year as accurately as possible, replenishment signals logically are much more accurate. Cycle counting supports this. There is a much-reduced opportunity for surprises, shortages, and the resulting MRP panic signals when inventory is maintained regularly as accurately as possible.

■ **Correct statement of assets** — When inventory record accuracy is not maintained, both the financial (book value) and the part number perpetual balances are less than reliable. If the financial books are inaccurate due to accumulated process variation, ugly surprises can happen at the end of the year in the form of inventory shrink when only a physical inventory is done. The cycle count process gives an organization a better chance of maintaining accuracy and keeping the financial books in synchronization with the perpetual balances.

The Objective of Cycle Counting

There are several objectives to cycle counting. These objectives include:

1. To maintain a focus on inventory accuracy
2. To verify accuracy/identify errors
3. To identify causes of errors
4. To correct conditions causing errors
5. To measure accuracy
6. To maintain a correct accounting of assets

Even though it is a cost-added activity, few organizations have been able to eliminate cycle counting completely.

These objectives are the basis for inventory accuracy efforts as well as cycle counting. These objectives should be well understood and clearly written into job descriptions of personnel responsible for the cycle counting activity. Making the general employee population aware of the importance of accuracy by including it as part of their yearly personal job objectives can help affect the culture in a positive way.

Cycle counting is a valuable part of an accuracy effort. Few organizations have been able to eliminate cycle counting completely.

ABC Stratification

Many organizations have cycle count processes developed and based on using an ABC stratification of the inventory. Organizations that have not yet utilized this approach should seriously consider it. It is simple to get started and to implement.

The first step in using ABC stratification is to have the item master or part number files stratified by value. This is normally done with factors that include:

- Monetary item value
- Item usage
- Criticality of an item in the manufacturing process
- Difficulty to procure

Most business systems have an equation for calculating the break points for inventory class assignment built into the software. All of the popular business system software packages have this ABC stratification feature, as do most of the less popular ones. The equation will typically ask for value cutoffs and volume factors in the setup of this feature. The Pareto principle is applied here. (The Pareto principle says that generally 80 percent of the impact will be caused by 20 percent of the factors.) This application of the Pareto principle results in some generally accepted patterns:

- **A items** — The top 10 to 15 percent of the monetary-value-based (cost per piece and usage volume) part numbers after stratification are often automatically assigned to the status of an A class item. These are items that require the most attention and investment in maintenance for accuracy. These are the items that have the biggest impact if errors in counts occur. Once the calculation is completed, most organizations also manually go through the item numbers to add and adjust according to additional knowledge. Most items that are critical or difficult to procure are added to the A item list. These criteria are not always easily sorted automatically.

Some materials managers are uncomfortable about doing this manual manipulation after the system finishes the calculation and report for A items. There is no reason to feel bad. Almost all companies do this and for good reason. The materials department is responsible for inventory control and material availability. Sometimes a straight calculation is not good enough to take into consideration other critical knowledge about the components.

- **C Items** — The lowest 60 to 80 percent of the value items (cost per piece and usage volume) can usually be assigned the status of C-classed items. On the reverse side of the scale from A items, C items are parts/materials that have low impact. Examples might be hardware or common fasteners. C items are usually not difficult to get with short notice, and these parts do not usually have a great amount of stock-on-hand value at any one time. These conditions minimize risk with C items. This is what makes C items candidates for less concentrated control.

- **B items** — The balance of the items are assigned as B items. B items will be reviewed and counted more frequently than C items and include items that are not in the A category of value but have more impact than low-impact C items. An example might be a lower cost colorant used in plastics blow molding that has a lead time of a week — low impact costwise, but could be a problem if requirements are not replenished in a timely manner for an order. Other examples would include items such as harnesses from the Far East that do not have great value but have long lead times. B item listing is for all items that are not critical or costly enough to be A items, but do not fit the C category either.

As you can see, the rules around ABC stratification are flexible for good reason. Every business has its own set of idiosyncrasies linked to part usage that affect the process of risk management in inventory control.

- **D items** — Some organizations have added a fourth category called D items. As a general rule, there really is no need for this extra category, but there is also no reason why it cannot be assigned if the materials manager feels strongly about it. D items are a subset of C items and are the really "cheap and dirty" components. For example, water is a component in the manufacture of some items. Water might be considered a D item in some environments where it is easily obtained and not too costly. Using D items is strictly your call. It is certainly not necessary.

To summarize stratification, most organizations use the enterprise resource planning (ERP) business computer software system to stratify their inventory into three or four categories, followed by some manual massaging according to impact other than just monetary value alone. Such impacts might include frequency of use, lead time, items that are rationed, criticality, etc.

> **T**o stratify their inventory, most organizations use their ERP software functionality. All of the leading software providers do an adequate job of this in their standard packages.

The association thought of first in stratification is link to the cycle counting process. There is a specific expectation for each category in terms of how frequently the cycle count checks would be done. The typical counting frequency in high-performance organizations is:

- **A items** — Counted every three months or four times a year
- **B items** — Counted every six months or twice a year
- **C (and D) items** — Counted once a year

A stated earlier, do not take lightly the impact to the business as a factor in this stratification assignment. The more effective stratification assignments also include impact to the business. For example, hardware can actually become an A item. If this hardware is specific to the application and comes from a supplier thousands of miles away, it becomes very critical. One organization in Shanghai provides a good example of this situation. Some low-cost hardware was only available from North America in a particular configuration and hardness. This item was labeled on the company's item master file as an A class item simply because it was not procured easily and a long lead time was required to ship it overseas. There are many other such examples of assigning stratification codes that do not exactly follow the generic computer equation.

The reasons for stratifying inventory include more than just cycle counting. Stratification plays an important part in determining safety stock, replenishment cycles, and review time required by planners. Materials replenishment policy is usually written around class stratification. For example, there could be a policy that A items should never reach levels of more than three days of on-hand inventory. In some automotive businesses, A items are ordered and delivered every hour with virtually no stock held beyond current manufacturing requirements.

High-performance organizations massage their stratification sorts according to the specific criticality of components in their environment.

It cannot be stated often enough that inventory stratification is an important component of good materials management. High-performance organizations do not blindly utilize the computer-generated equations for stratifying inventory. They feel free to massage the results of the sort according to criticality of components in their environment.

Measuring Inventory Location Balance Accuracy

Measuring accuracy is an integral part of cycle counting. Accuracy is measured by:

- Actual part number
- Actual location
- Actual count in that location

as compared to

- Record of part number
- Record of location
- Record of balance in that location

There are tolerance levels that are generally accepted as minimum standards of acceptability, but the use of these levels is not necessarily synonymous with high performance. Many world-class organizations are going beyond the minimum definition of accuracy and completely eliminating tolerances for accuracy performance metrics. While the latter is desirable, many processes are not yet up to that "no tolerance" expectation.

Step one for organizations just starting to get serious about inventory record accuracy should focus first on Class A ERP minimum standards and move to world-class later.

Minimally Acceptable Class A ERP Certifiable Process

A items	±0 percent
B items	±2 percent
C items	±3 to 5 percent depending on application and cost

The Five Steps to Cycle Counting

1. **Measure starting point and post the measurement visibly** — By day 45, the initial performance reading should be well understood and posted. This not only gives everyone an understanding of the opportunity available when performance is below 95+ percent, but also shows progress once activity begins. The performance signs should be big enough to be visible from several yards away (Figure 9-1), at minimum a standard-size sheet of paper readable from twenty-five feet away. Often this creates incentive among departments or storerooms to improve accuracy levels. It also creates an opportunity for managers (especially top managers) to ask questions about the accuracy as they walk through the facility. This will happen more often if there are signs posted like the one illustrated. In more advanced settings, managers have posted signs with photos of the process owners to increase the feeling of ownership and accountability. Use your imagination.

2. **Education and training** — In Chapters 1, 2, and 3, education was discussed and its importance underlined. It is imperative to have people with high levels of understanding if the cycle counting program is to be effective. This can only happen through proper education as described in earlier chapters. Education needs to be delivered by knowl-

> **S**upervisors make some of the best instructors. They set a good example and become especially well versed themselves. This makes it easier for them to set a proper example for others.

Raw Material
Warehouse

95%

Week of 07/12/xx

Figure 9-1. Sample performance board.

edgeable people who are enthusiastic about the process and expected results. Management must also be involved with the education for it to be fully effective. Line managers and supervisors are some of the best people to be trained for this delivery. By having them deliver the training, they become trained especially well themselves.

3. **Control group A** — A prerequisite to beginning the cycle counting process is having a good understanding of root cause and having process controls in place that eliminate these barriers to high performance. The control group methodology orchestrates the detection and elimination of errors by a process of counting a number of frequently used locations every day (same locations) to detect errors within twenty-four hours from when they occurred. (Details of this action are provided in Chapter 5.)

4. **Control group B** — Once the first control group (control group A) is at 100 percent accuracy for ten consecutive days, it is recommended that a second test group be initiated for verification of process control. The second control group uses the same techniques as the first, except a new set of locations and parts/items is counted. This new control group (control group B) also should be proven by demonstrating ten consecutive error-free days as well. (See Chapter 5 for details.)

> Ten consecutive days of 100 percent accuracy measured in the control group is a good sign that your process, at least for the control group, is now in control.

5. **Cycle counting** — Cycle counting is the process of complete site location counts scheduled over predetermined time periods. Location counts are scheduled each day or each week, resulting in a periodic complete check. (For example, when ABC stratification is used as the cycle count base, often A class items are counted once a quarter-year, B items once a half-year, and C items once a year.) Cycle counting ensures that the accurate controlled processes developed while finding and eliminating root cause and reacting to the control group findings are, in fact, maintained. Sustainability is important or the process control work done prior to this step is lost.

Scheduling the Cycle Count Process

Once a full-scale cycle counting program is in place, it should be expected that all items will be touched at some time, at least once, during the year by a cycle counter.

Table 9-2.   Cycle Count Capacity Planning and Schedule Matrix

Item Stratification	Counts per Year	Quantity of Items	Total Counts Required
A	4	150	600
B	2	150	300
C	1	700	700
Total counts for year			1600

Let's look at an example of a cycle count schedule: There is a 1000-part-number overall database. The ABC stratification in this sample company (see Table 9-2) resulted in the following quantities per level:

> 1000 total items
> 150 A items
> 150 B items
> 700 C items

Here, A items might get counted once a quarter. This means cycle counters would have to count 150 items four times or 600 counts of A items in a year's time period. This would amount to 2.4 counts for A items per workday using 250 workdays as a base. Continuing with the math, a chart could be developed to schedule and understand capacity issues associated with the cycle counting process.

With 1600 counts required per year, the amount per day (1600 divided by 250) is 6.4 counts per day. This can now be scheduled and become part of the regular work requirements of the stores areas. Some of these counts may be in nonwarehouse areas and will be assigned to people responsible for these location balances.

Who Does the Cycle Counts?

Often the people accountable for cycle counting are the people in the area that handle the inventory. In some organizations, this can be the workers who weld/assemble/kit the components. In others, it is stores employees who service the assembly areas. Regardless of who it is, there are some simple requirements for these people to qualify for the duties of cycle counting (Table 9-3).

Table 9-3. What Cycle Counters Need to Know

- Knowledge of how and where material is stored
- Knowledge of location identifiers and the stores layout
- Know how to identify items and be authorized/able to get access to drawings and specifications as needed
- Knowledge of the transaction flow and reporting processes
- Be aware of any cutoff control* requirements if they exist
- Knowledge of how to access the on-line system for problem solving and reconciliation
- Knowledge of the S&OP procedures and how to access them

* Cutoff times may exist in operations with transactions that are batched and processed sometime after the actual event of inventory transfer. Cutoffs can also be an issue in operations that automatically trigger transactions from other specific events such as a transaction confirming a completed assembly or the receipt of a part in production.

The cycle counters' activity will vary from day to day as they encounter variation in data accuracy, but there is a general expectation of process that can and should be documented.

The Typical Steps in the Process

Get Assignment of Daily Counts

This may be assigned from a dispatcher or manager, or the cycle counters may generate the list by accessing the computer themselves. Some of the cycle counts may not be generated from cycle count software, but instead may be the result of planners or others requesting location checks. These additional counts should be included in the cycle count process even though they may skew performance results downward.

Prepare the Cycle Counting Form

Typically, there is a form that lists the parts to be counted and the locations to check. No quantities/balances should be listed on this form at this point. This can influence the count accuracy. Counters tend to stop counting when they have reached the perpetual count if they know what it is, especially if they are at the end of a row or box, etc. Called "blind counting," high-performance organizations always hand out only the part number and location(s) for the cycle count. This just keeps everyone honest and the process much more pure.

Perform the Cycle Count

There are only a few actions that a cycle counter is expected to perform during his or her duties. All of them are equally important and should be part of the documented process used for training the cycle counters:

- Inspect the items for errors.
  1. Is it the right item — does it match the specifications as can be determined by sight?
  2. If they are supposed to be "right hand," are they?
  3. Are there any parts that spill over into adjoining locations that are not logged with the correct location?
- Evaluate the cleanliness and orderliness of each location.
  1. Observe the area for mixed parts in the location from other adjoining locations.
  2. Check for damaged items.
  3. Is there contamination such as dirt or heavy dust that might affect item quality?
  4. Is the location properly labeled and is the label easily seen from the floor?

Total the Counts for All Locations

Counting all locations in the area can often be helpful for location/ transaction problem solving later. If there are locations in other buildings or long distances from the location picked for cycle count, use judgment before automatically counting all locations. The idea is not to create work, but to make sure accuracy is assured.

Check the Database for Count Accuracy of Each Location

The check can be done by the cycle counter or can be done by the dispatcher. In many organizations, a dispatcher does the book check and posts the accuracy later after confirmation. Some organizations are not large enough to have this luxury.

Recount as Necessary Any Discrepancies

Any time there is a discrepancy in the cycle count as compared to the perpetual, a second audit should be done right away.

Any time there is a mismatch between the cycle count and perpetual record, a second count should be assigned right away. This makes it important to check the balance records as soon as possible after the cycle counts are completed.

Determine Root Cause of the Discrepancy

Determining the facts leading to root cause may require investigatory work utilizing transaction reports, audit trails, and historical files as well as questioning people who may have accessed this location. This work is not always done by the cycle counter. Some larger organizations have an inventory specialist that performs the root cause analysis to determine the reason for error. This specialist does not have to be a full-time position. It could even be the storekeeper or warehouse team leader. Regardless, there should be someone designated to ensure that this function and responsibility are clearly defined and predictable.

Root cause can be elusive, but the analyst needs to be voracious in his or her search for the truth. This investigatory work should be considered top priority, especially with reoccurring errors in specific areas of the warehouse. Without knowing the root cause, the fixes are not easily administered.

Logging the reason code "unknown" should be a very serious last resort and should be avoided if at all possible.

Sometimes root cause is not known and there are few or no clues. Because this is a fact, it can easily become a regular assumption that there is no background information available. Do not make this assumption quickly. Some organizations have been known to require manager approval before a reason code can be logged as "unknown."

Generate Corrective Actions

Corrective actions are the key to the elimination of inaccuracy in inventory records. Actions can only be driven if there are well-understood root cause facts. It is not unusual for this rigor to go against the culture of an organization during the first stages of implementation. Because of this, this

> **C**orrective actions are the key to sustainable inventory record accuracy.

process expectation may require education sessions or communication with individuals involved with the corrective actions. Sometimes, for example, there might be an opinion that corrective actions are to be done after the normal work is completed. This attitude ensures that corrective action will always have a low priority and often will not be accomplished in a timely manner. This is not acceptable. Corrective action needs to be part of the "normal work."

Again, these actions may not be generated by the cycle counter, depending on the organization size and management wishes. Usually the person responsible for determining the root cause will also generate the corrective actions.

Post Results

The accuracy should be posted separately in each controlled inventory area in the facility. Making sure that the results are easily seen and understood is also important. This posting should be in a high-traffic area and the daily posting should have numbers at least ten inches high. Using a standard sheet of paper with the number taking up most of it is a good guideline for posting accuracy numbers in each area.

Update Inventory Records to the Corrected Balances

Updating the perpetual inventory records can have an effect on the finances of the company, so it should be highly regarded as a critical process. These adjustments may require authorization for balance adjustments outside of certain limits (see the section on location balance adjustment authorization later in this chapter).

Regardless of who is authorized to do the changes to balances, a summary report should go to management each day. As an example of what can be done, one manufacturing facility in Montreal, Quebec, coded the software in its ERP system to create an audible "buzz" on the computer terminal in the materials manager's office every time an inventory adjustment transaction was made. The noise was triggered by a specific adjustment transaction. It kept the manager well aware of transaction frequency!

Begin Collecting "Call-In" Balance Audit Request List

Organizations always have variation that drives count requests. Good process accuracy only limits the need, but seldom completely eliminates it. A call-in list should be established for nonemergency item counts and can be integrated with the computer-generated list for tomorrow's cycle count. More critical counts may need to be done right away and would be included in today's cycle count assignments and results.

Document

The preceding cycle count activities should be documented in the form of a process map and standard operating procedures describing the exceptions to the procedures and how the cycle counter should deal with these exceptions. This becomes a helpful tool in instructing new cycle counters and maintaining consistency with experienced ones.

When computer-driven cycle count formats are not available in the business system software to count A, B, and C items periodically, spreadsheet versions are often developed. As stated earlier, some organizations periodically designate areas to be counted completely, resulting in the same frequency of counts as would an ABC setup. For example, some warehouses are counted twice a year by having X number of locations counted each day starting on the east side and working toward the west.

Other ways to determine cycle count items/locations that are less desirable are listed below. They are less desirable because predictability of count frequency is less scientific. However, these are acceptable alternatives when computer help is not easily available. Examples of these are:

1. When reorder is needed, cycle count the existing location if there is one. If not, verify zero balance.
2. When a replenishment order is received, cycle count the existing location if there is one. If not, verify zero balance.
3. When the balance is at zero, check if a location is still listed. If there is a location, cycle count it.
4. When a record is negative, this should always be cycle counted since it is obviously wrong. This is a no-brainer and is part of good

material management even with a good cycle count process. There is no such thing in reality as a negative balance. These odd records are a call for help that should be heeded!

5. When the stock picker empties a location, check to see if the location shows zero after the pick. This is a great time to check, especially if random location system strategy is used and locations are always zeroed out. Again, this is a practice that should be done regardless of the method of cycle counting. By placing a ticket in the bottom of each location at the time parts are put away, this check is made easily. The stock picker simply needs to pull the ticket at the time of the last part pull and hand it in to the dispatcher as a verification of a zeroed location.

6. When there is a quantity on hand but no location, this is another obvious error and should create a red flag for cycle count as soon as it happens. It is impossible to have parts with no location, and anything that is stated as a fact and is impossible is an accuracy gem to be mined.

Being Organized

Having parts stored in proper containers and having them properly labeled helps the cycle counters do their job effectively and efficiently. Many times, odd-shaped parts can be stored in specially built pallets that make it very easy to see how many there are in the location.

When parts are small and require protective packaging, special considerations should be made to have packaging that is easy to count and pick for production use. This might mean packaging in egg-carton-type layers that force consistent amounts per layer or packaging items in dozens or, even better, for counting, tens. Be aware of the dangers when packaging multiple parts in one package. The packaging must be as foolproof as possible so that people do not pick a box of ten and think they are picking one item.

> Having parts properly packaged and labeled makes cycle counting much easier, more efficient, and more accurate.

Lastly, have the location identifiers well labeled and easy to see and read. Make sure these labels are consistently applied throughout the entire facility. Label locations so that they can be read from any direction.

Table 9-4. Adjustment Authorization: Written Approval Must Be Received from the Following People Prior to Having the Database Adjusted

	Variance from Any Verified Cycle Count			
Adjustments Made	0–250	251–2000	2001–15,000	15,001+
CFO				X
Plant Manager			X	
Materials Manager			X	
Stockroom Manager		X		
Accuracy Analyst	X			

Location Balance Adjustment Authorization

In many organizations, adjustments to inventory over certain perimeters require specific authorization. This is just good policy to project the priority over asset management and the need for accuracy in data. Management should be intimately involved when a process begins to deviate from designed process control points, especially when it involves the financial statements and balance sheet.

In some organizations, the cycle count analyst might have the authority to adjust inventory as much as $250 per item. Adjustments reaching $251 might require the stockroom manager to approve the transaction and, accordingly, very large adjustments may require the chief financial officer's authorization. With each level of authority in the organization, a new level of accuracy concern is raised. This type of process control also keeps those in management in the loop when they may not be due to workload and normal distractions. Where your organization determines to draw the lines of limitation is up to the management of your organization. An example is shown in Table 9-4.

Recently, in a class I taught in Minnesota, the attendees were especially attentive during the discussion about adjustment authorization. When asked if they had a policy like this authorizing adjustments, the controller quickly answered "yes." There was an unusual silence from the rest of the class and I suspected some learning was about to happen. In just a few minutes of additional quizzing, it came out that they did have a policy, but nobody followed it on the floor. This was a surprise to the controller. Too often, this is the case in organizations.

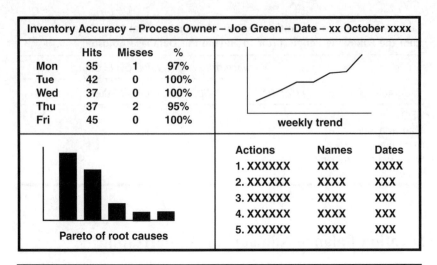

Figure 9-2. Quad chart for reporting and accountability.

Error Analysis — Weekly Performance Review

Simply having management sign off on the adjustment is not enough. Analysis of the error trends needs to be documented and distributed. The best way to demonstrate the trend is with a quadrant reporting format. This quadrant reporting format is the preferred form for reporting at the weekly performance review, a meeting held in all Class A ERP organizations to drive change and continuous improvement (see the example in Figure 9-2).

The weekly performance review meeting might best be held on Tuesday afternoon to review the performance of the preceding week. Each process owner reports the performance and actions driven from this process to the rest of the operations management staff. Inventory accuracy is just one of the measurements reported. Other metrics normally reported in this format are:

- Schedule adherence
- Schedule stability
- Bill of material accuracy
- Routing record accuracy
- Item master accuracy
- Procurement process accuracy

- Shop floor accuracy
- First-time quality
- Customer service

The weekly performance review process is an integral part of a robust management system that allows management to be involved in the follow-up of process control on a regular and predictable schedule. It helps establish accountability for process ownership. Without it, process ownership has little or no real meaning to the organization and will not be effective.

> The weekly performance review process is an extremely important management system element in high-performance businesses.

By using this type of form for reporting progress and performance, the organization becomes consistent and effective at problem solving and continuous improvement. It should be used consistently for all performance metrics including data accuracy.

Agenda

The weekly performance review meeting should be predictable and repeatable. This means that the meeting should be held the same time every week unless there is a holiday on that particular day. The agenda should be simple. Each process owner, including the inventory accuracy process owner, reports his or her progress for last week. Progress includes all elements on the quad chart explained in the next few pages. Questions are appropriate from the other team members if the process owner is not reporting performance to acceptable levels. The objective is not to hang anyone, but to offer help instead. Help can be in the form of resource, ideas, change in handoffs, etc.

Quad Chart

Top Left of Quad Chart

In the top left-hand quadrant, the daily cycle count performance is reported along with the weekly overall performance. It should consistently be reported as a daily performance and as a weekly totaled performance number.

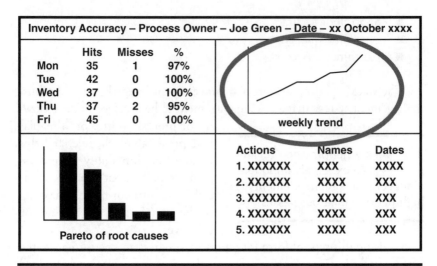

Figure 9-3.   Quad chart for reporting and accountability: trend chart.

Top Right of Quad Chart

The trend chart is displayed in the top right-hand quadrant (Figure 9-3). This is important to determine if the process is affecting the performance positively. If only the performance for the current period is reported, it is not clear if progress is being accomplished successfully.

Bottom Left of Quad Chart

A Pareto chart showing the reasons for misses will allow the organization to focus energy and resources on the most important barriers to successful accuracy. This is important in the beginning when accuracy is often being affected by many sources. The best organizations focus resources on the worst root causes that allow the biggest return for their investment. It is in this quadrant where the biggest challenges will come as the culture migrates. Process owners often will struggle with the definition of root cause. Management will have to combat "categories" versus real root cause. As has been said so many times prior, without root cause it is impossible to really eliminate the variation causing inaccuracies in the inventory balances.

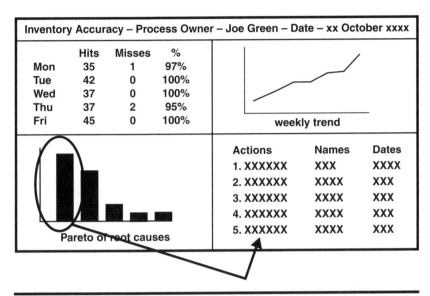

Figure 9-4. Quad chart for reporting and accountability: the root cause needs to be aligned with the actions taken.

Bottom Right of Quad Chart

Process improvement comes only by driving change through actions. By institutionalizing the action process and reporting it, follow-up is much more systematic and predictable. The root cause bar at the left side of the Pareto chart should have actions easily linked on the right-hand side of the quad chart (Figure 9-4).

As they start this new discipline level, many organizations are not prepared to delve into problem solving or root cause analysis to the depth required. Getting to root cause is sometimes helped by a simple 5-why exercise. Asking "why" five times greatly increases the likelihood of getting to the root cause of an opportunity.

The following is a list of common "symptoms" or "excuses." They are closer to categories than examples of root cause:

1. Counting error
2. Recording error
3. Identification error

4. Quality control error
5. Physical security breach
6. Supplier shipment error
7. Timing issue

The next list might better suit a list of root causes experienced in an inventory accuracy focus:

1. Improper training of cycle count personnel
2. Inadequate process to catch supplier shipment errors
3. Procedure not followed, new employee not trained
4. Computer software problem — it does not work like everybody thought it would
5. Parts not clearly labeled as having five in a bag or box

In the first list (excuses), it is not clear what actions to take. That still has to be determined from the real cause. It is an indicator that "why" has not been asked enough times to get to the actionable cause. The second list more easily positions the problem solver to direct specific activities to eliminate the root cause and improve the performance of the process. Actions can be linked and tracked to these causes.

During the weekly performance review meeting, process owners need to keep focused on root cause and not excuses. This will drive proper corrective actions and will reduce the cost needed to eliminate the barriers to high performance. Management has to play a role in this if it is to become a required behavior and a predictable component of the management system.

Timely Reporting of Cycle Counts

There is a model hierarchy in the reporting and measuring of data accuracy for high performance:

- **Daily** — Inventory accuracy is a daily measurement and should therefore be reported and displayed visually each day in the work area. This would be posted by the dispatcher or person in charge of coordinating the cycle counting effort.
- **Weekly** — Weekly performance summaries are reported at the weekly performance review meeting held early in the week (usually

Table 9-5. Performance Metric

| | Performance Month | | | | | | | | | | | |
Owner	J	F	M	A	M	J	J	A	S	O	N	D
Master Schedule D Smith	95											
Schedule Stability J Jones	93											
1st-Time Quality B Smith	92											
Bill of Material Accuracy J. Green	99											
Inventory Accuracy D Sheldon	98											
Procurement R McBee	97											
Shop Floor J Bollinger	98											
Customer Service J Evans	98											

on Tuesdays) at the same time each week. This information would be gathered by the process owner and reported along with the appropriate actions at this management system event.

- **Monthly** — Monthly reporting should be distributed and posted in the cafeteria, office area, and the factory. A good way to display this information is with a measurement board that covers all the performance metrics for the company. High-performance companies may have as many as fifteen to twenty measurements reported at this visual level to increase awareness and drive improvement in areas including customer service, warrantee, quality, schedule adherence, changeover improvements, process improvements, and data accuracy. On wall charts like the one shown in Table 9-5 used for Class A ERP implementations, percentage numbers, representing performance as an accuracy percentage of plan to actual, are displayed in the columns as is shown in the inventory accuracy performance for January. In this case, inventory was 98 percent accurate. Many organizations have fabricated such performance charts out of simple white boards purchased from office supply outlets. With vinyl letter and number decals and automotive striping, they can be transformed into professional-looking performance boards quite quickly and with little expense.

Cutoff Times

There are system designs where cutoff times become a factor in cycle counting due to the timing of transactions in the system. In these environments, caution needs to be taken to assure accurate cycle counting processes.

- **Batch processing** — Some organizations still use batch processing. This is a system constraint where transactions are collected and, at a scheduled time, a designated person or position processes several transactions at one time (thus the name "batch"). This is not usually desirable given a choice, but for an organization with no alternative but to administer batch processing, cutoff times play an especially important part in the cycle count reconciliation process.
- **Backflushing** — Some organizations use backflushing (auto-deduct transactions) triggered from another transaction. Since the timing of these transactions usually does not agree with the actual movement of inventory, cutoff times are also a factor here. Backflushing can cause a lot of headaches associated with cycle counting and usually is avoided except where absolutely necessary for cost efficiencies, such as in work in process.

The establishment of cutoff times requires process recognition of these timing issues and education and training for people to deal with them. If the company has a batch system with no option of changing it, the rules are usually quite simple:

1. Count during nonoperational times. If the batch is sequential with the cycle count, less reconciliation time is required. Sometimes it makes sense to have cycle counting done on alternative shifts outside normal working hours (Figure 9-5).
2. Count at the end or start of the shift to minimize activity. This is sometimes the only answer in operations where the work schedule is nonstop, around the clock. Many operations today are scheduled 24/7. Again, if the batch is scheduled with the optimization of cycle counting in mind, reconciliation time can be minimized. Sometimes simply holding documents until after the cycle count is helpful.

In reality, maybe neither of these situations is perfect or ideal. The ideal system design isolates controlled areas and transactions are processed as

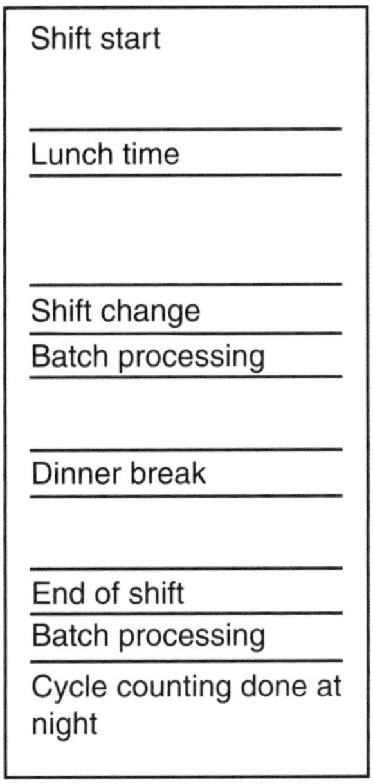

```
┌─────────────────────────────┐
│  Shift start                │
│  ─────────────              │
│  Lunch time                 │
│  ─────────────              │
│  Shift change               │
│  ─────────────              │
│  Batch processing           │
│  ─────────────              │
│  Dinner break               │
│  ─────────────              │
│  End of shift               │
│  ─────────────              │
│  Batch processing           │
│  ─────────────              │
│  Cycle counting done at     │
│  night                      │
└─────────────────────────────┘
```

Figure 9-5. Shift and cycle counting scheduling during a workday.

material is moved from the controlled stores area. Today, most high-performance organizations do not use batch processing. In these organizations, cycle count timing is an even more important issue.

In environments where transactions are real time, the cutoff becomes a real challenge. In many of these situations, the only answer is to do things quickly at shift change and schedule the counts at the shift time with the least expected activity. For example, many times there is less material movement on the midnight shift than in the daytime. In this case, the right time to do the transaction would be at the start of the midnight shift.

In environments where transactions are real time, cutoffs can be a real challenge. Optimum times must be scheduled for cycle counts.

If your organization has an open shift for preventative maintenance, does not schedule the weekends, or has some open time between shifts or at lunchtime, these become opportunities for cycle count cutoffs. Only you can figure out the best time for your operation. The common denominator is that the best time is always the time with the least transaction activity. No transaction activity, if available sometime during the day, offers the optimum scheduling opportunity.

Cycle Counting Work in Process

The cycle counting described in this chapter so far has dealt with "controlled" storage areas throughout the factory and process where inventory is, either by process design or habit, normally stored for more than twenty-four hours. There is also inventory frequently held briefly in work in process (WIP).

The factors affecting count accuracy in WIP deal more with yield and, in very rare cases, pilferage. Scrap and/or yield must be reported precisely and in a timely manner for WIP balances to remain accurate. Because of the speed at which these transactions are required and the normal priority of assemblers and other production workers, sometimes these transactions do not get processed in a timely manner. In fact, in some organizations these transactions often do not get processed at all!

In an ideal situation, there would normally be:

1. A manual (nonbackflush) transaction processed as inventory moves into WIP
2. A short process cycle time of less than a day
3. A (nonbackflush) transaction is done as inventory is moved into the finished goods area

When this situation exists, WIP cycle counts are rarely required. Instead, a WIP balance reconciliation should happen at least once a week. These reconciliations would be concerned with negative balances, unplanned trends in inventory value either up or down, excessive inventory in a few part numbers, etc. Unfortunately, all situations are not ideal.

In situations where high or consistent yields have yet to be demonstrated or proven, or where process cycle times are longer than a day, WIP areas may require cycle counting. I often try to avoid this except to clear or check a suspected problem simply because it is almost impossible to accurately cycle count a WIP balance, especially when work is going on. Cycle counting in this context is the confirmation of order quantity of good parts on the factory floor in process. "Good" in this discussion would be defined as inventory matching the specification required at that point in the process.

When WIP cycle counting is administered in a facility, these counting results should be reported separately from the controlled area cycle counts. The posting should be visual, and the same educational and training needs are imperative. The objectives and measurements are the same for WIP as in the controlled area cycle count process. Just substitute work order (or order quantity in a repetitive environment) and routing step in place of the "location" verification in the controlled area cycle counting process. This combination of work order and routing step replaces the location record in WIP.

In your organization, if WIP does not travel rapidly or if there is not a continuous workforce, you may decide to cycle count and publish WIP balances. If there is anything controversial in data accuracy, this is it. Some will say that not to cycle count any of the company's asset inventory is a sin. I will not argue with them. I am just trying to make sure this text is as realistic as possible and conveys what high-performance organizations really do. You must make up your own mind.

> **S**ome will say that not to cycle count WIP is a sin. Do not get caught arguing against them.

Cycle Counting Long Term

Many people believe cycle counting is a value-added activity. This is curious, since most of these same people quickly will agree that a similar topic, quality inspection, is a cost-added activity. If inspecting a manufacturing process midstream or inspecting a received component from a supplier is cost added, is cycle counting any different?

The opportunity for organizations to go beyond cycle counting is real. If after several months the process of inventory accuracy continues to be in control, as evidenced by high-performance accuracy during cycle count checks, it can be prudent to cut back on the frequency of counts. Audits will, however, probably always be required to assure process control is ongoing. Audits are the verification monitoring process of required controls. While cycle counting is not truly a value-added activity, it is an important and major step in moving an organization closer to record accuracy.

This has been a long and important chapter. Use the information as a guide to establish the practices and documentation in your organization. At this point in the process, your organization should have gained some important percentage points toward accuracy of inventory records. It's time for some fun!

It is time to have some fun! Start planning the celebrations.

10

Day 90: Celebration Number One!

Day 90

By day 90, the process will have been defined and controlled. The documentation will be complete to this point in the process improvement strategy and people will have been trained in the use of procedures. Cycle counting will be auditing process control and the performance should be improving significantly. Most of the new variation seen now should be from the initial physical inventory and will begin to disappear as the cycle count makes its way through the entire inventory. When the performance meter moves beyond 90 percent, it is time to celebrate!

Why Celebrate Now?

Celebrating is one of the best ways to educate. People take a strong signal from top management when management gets excited about certain behaviors. In a celebration, top management gets to show enthusiasm about having the company's very important asset, inventory records, controlled accurately. The bigger the noise is during celebration, the bigger the population of employees that will hear the message. Time for lots of noise! Bring on my favorite — pizza with the works!

Some managers feel 90 percent is not worth celebrating. If starting from 80 percent or below, 90 percent accuracy is a good time to send a signal to the team that this is still important. Celebrations are part of the education process.

Some managers will think at this point (90 percent accuracy) that the goal of accuracy really has not been obtained and therefore feel uncomfortable about celebrating an accuracy achievement. They are right in a sense because, after all, 95+ percent is the real goal.

In most storerooms, especially large warehouses with a lot of items and locations, it is as challenging to move or improve accuracy from a sustained 95 percent to a sustained 97 percent (two points) as it is to get it from 85 percent to 95 percent (ten points). This is because once the low-hanging fruit or easy root causes are harvested, the job gets more challenging. The errors at this point just do not happen as often to allow for detection and elimination. Sometimes the causes are elusive and difficult to determine as well.

In most organizations starting from poor discipline, 90 percent, although not high performance by any means, is a significant achievement worth celebrating. By taking this opportunity, you get to underline the significance of data accuracy to the organization and maybe reach more people who have not achieved that level of thought leadership yet. Besides, who wants to miss an opportunity for pizza?!

Ideas for Celebration

There are many different ideas used for celebrating Class A ERP milestone achievements. Here are just a few. Included are ideas beyond what might be appropriate for the achievement of 90 percent inventory accuracy to help stimulate the creative juices. Celebration ideas are limited only by lack of imagination and creativity. Have fun with it! You will notice that there is a common denominator in many of these ideas — food. Rich Curtis, the sales manager at The Raymond Corporation's Parts Distribution Center in Syracuse, New York, while I was general manager there, respectfully used to accuse me of only thinking about food every time we had an opportunity for celebration. Guilty as charged!

- Management cooks hot dogs and hamburgers on the grill outside and serves the workforce on a longer-than-normal lunch hour. This is also an opportunity for a communication session and associated education beyond the message of the accuracy reward.

- Pizza is brought in by the truckload and everyone has an extra-long lunch hour. Again, combine it with an educational communication session and a few accolades.

- Time is scheduled in an auditorium or large area and a customer is asked to talk to the workforce about gains seen from the process improvement. (Hey — no food involved with this one!)

- One plant manager in Boston took a large group out for a lobster dinner. Their celebration happened to be for setup reduction gains, but it could work in any goal situation. (Ah, that's better — back to food.)

- A dance-costume manufacturer in Pennsylvania used to celebrate a successful seasonal-cycle completion with an off-campus education session. It was a chance to recuperate from the highly seasonal demand cycle and to learn something at the same time. This is especially creative because it positioned education as a celebration event.

- One manufacturer in upstate Greene, New York, would sometimes have fresh cider and doughnuts brought in for everyone for celebrations that fell in the autumn months. This was always a treat.

- One time, I was part of a celebration in France that included wine in the plant. That idea may not sell as well in Kansas, however.

- Walnut plaques, the kind with the certificates and Plexiglas pinned over the front, are very exciting for employees, especially when awarded in front of the entire employee base.

- One plant manager in Syracuse, New York, used to award employees with one-day seminars held downtown in the fancier hotels. By watching the mail, he would look for appropriate topics, presenters, and times to send employees. Many of these shop-level employees felt honored to have the company spend money for their educational use and enjoyed the change it provided in routine. The knowledge was a bonus for everyone!

- In some venues, it can be appropriate to have the vending machines for drinks and snacks opened up for the day, with the bill going to the company instead of the employees.

- The employees always welcome time off. One company in Cincinnati allowed departments with the best process control to earn time-off credits. These were added to existing vacation benefits. This celebration vehicle needs to be administered carefully, as it can become a perceived obligation/benefit. It can also become an emotional issue if not administered fairly. I include it only as food for thought.

■ Many companies have box seats at the local stadium or arena that they use for entertaining customers. These can make a wonderful reward for employees as well when not in use for customers. Too many times, they are distributed only among the elite in the company. This offers a very special opportunity to reward employees for a job well done.

■ Fill in this line with your new idea.

There are many ways to celebrate successfully. Notice that no monetary rewards are suggested. Experience has shown that when money is involved, people start to connive ways to increase their return and often lose focus on the real goal. Monetary rewards have their place for commissions in sales departments or certainly for overall job performance, but not for rewarding process improvement. In the wrong applications, money often can cause more problems than it is worth. It can become a demotivational factor as easily as it can motivate.

One particular situation I was involved with in Detroit that combined money with rewarding behavior changes ended up in fights between employees. Too many people were worried about the award rather than the process because they often thought somebody else was getting some sort of advantage over them. They even held back ideas when they thought they would not get top billing for the period. When "nasty lucre" gets involved, it sometimes becomes a new ball game. My experience has taught me to avoid money as a reward in inventory accuracy when possible and not just because it is cheaper to avoid it.

> **E**xcept in specific applications, monetary rewards are not always helpful. Often, they actually deter good behavior. Celebrations and recognition have worked best in my experience.

The one exception to this rule is for rewarding management behavior and then it should be for longer term performance, not event driven. When management's bonuses are calculated around inventory record accuracy, it usually finds its way to the top of the priority list. That is always a good thing.

Is This the First or Only Time to Celebrate?

If the company situation or starting point was so bad that it feels appropriate at day 80 to celebrate 80 percent accuracy, go for it! Small celebrations (such as someone bringing in a cake) for the cycle counting crew or inventory accuracy team are very appropriate on the way to 95 percent performance levels.

In our studies, we have found that the average accuracy for organizations that have not made inventory accuracy a focus is around 60 percent. Your starting point may be quite different. Every plant/distribution center has to consider its starting point, but a good suggestion is to use the following inventory accuracy celebration schedule as a standard for reference if the starting point is 60 percent accuracy or lower:

80 percent	small celebration
90 percent	Bigger Celebration
95 percent	BIG CELEBRATION
98 percent	PULL OUT THE STOPS!

Keep in mind that these celebration points assume sustainable performance levels and not just one-time anomalies. If there is a question about sustainability, hold off the celebration for a few weeks. For lower reward points, sometimes four consecutive weeks of performance is reassuring enough. As reward points are raised, more proof may be called for. At Class A levels of performance, for example, usually a three-month performance period is required to prove sustainability of process. Full Class A levels of performance include schedule adherence and customer service metrics.

> **S**ustainability is a consideration when planning celebrations. Usually a few weeks is time enough to increase confidence in the on-going process.

11

Measurement of Inventory Location Balance Record Accuracy

This chapter reviews the technical points of performance measurement, what to expect, how to communicate it properly, how to report it, and what the mechanics are in the measurement process itself.

Phases of Performance Measurement

Performance measurement in high-performance organizations is not "something they do"; it is "the way they think." Typically, there is not a great desire to measure performance in the beginning stages of implementation. As is human nature, people often see this change as a threat to their security or even a violation of their honor or trust. They are likely to think: "Why do you want to measure my performance anyway?" or "Do you not trust me or do you think I am not doing appropriate work?" This is the first phase of performance measurement. There are three.

> **P**eople often see measurements as threatening or even a violation of their honor or trust.

In my experience, there are stages people go through when first being introduced to performance metrics. The stages usually would look like the following:

- **Stage 1**— "It's not me you need to measure, it's him/her." (Points finger at another employee.) This is probably the denial stage.
- **Stage 2** — "Okay, I guess you're (management) not going to forget this crazy idea. What was it you wanted measured anyway?" This is the acknowledgment stage — it is real.
- **Stage 3** — "I have been measuring this and I found that there are some other diagnostic indicators that will help in the elimination of the root cause of the variation." This is the exciting stage — the stage of discovery.

Obviously, education plays a part in this transition; practice does as well. Management must send a clear and consistent message that the measures are about process and not people. This is done through both actions and words. Management's signal cannot be delegated to the staff. The employees watch and know!

Many companies today are surprisingly still at 50 percent location balance accuracy. When organizations address the situation, they find it is not people that have to be addressed first, it is always the process. People always do what the norm of expectation is.

If the speed limit on a freeway is a certain speed, but is not closely monitored or is enforced at speeds considerably higher, and there is not a present and obvious danger, most people will naturally do the maximum the process will allow.

This is exactly what happens in the factory and warehouse. People do not see the dangers of taking shortcuts. Many times, they actually think they are helping the cause by reacting to a customer request and shortcutting the paperwork or transaction process. Management even sometimes rewards this "hero" behavior.

Management even rewards short-cuts, calling it "heroism." All of a sudden, the norms need to change and management needs to set the stage.

In these cases, it is the processes, not the people, that are the problem. After all, people are somewhat predictable. It is the measurement process that creates the necessary feedback.

The measurement of data accuracy is a high-level measurement. It generally is not a measure that indicates root cause. Data accuracy measurements are what might be referred to as a "barometric measure." This term initially was used in the mid-1980s by Bob Shearer, a friend and very effective master scheduling manager at The Raymond Corporation in Greene, New York, to describe the Class A measurements.

Barometric Versus Diagnostic Measures

There are data accuracy metrics that are by and large generic and would be classed as barometric measures. These measures let management know whether or not a "storm front" is coming. These metrics are the same in every business regardless of product.

Barometric data accuracy measures include accuracy indicators such as:

- Inventory location balance accuracy
- Bills of material accuracy
- Routing record accuracy
- Standards accuracy
- Item master record accuracy

In each case, there are specifics that become important indicators of process variation causes. Without the high-level Class A ERP metrics in place, it is difficult to globally manage the predictability of the many processes utilizing information from these databases.

Below the Class A measures is another level of measurement utilized to determine root cause for variability. These measurements are known as the diagnostic measures and are designed to smoke out the real reasons why inaccuracies exist when they do. Examples of diagnostic measures might include:

- Percent of accurate counts received from suppliers
- "Issue" transaction accuracy of each separate controlled inventory storage area
- Pick accuracy per picker
- Number of minus or negative balances per week
- Number of "surprise" shortages in assembly indicating pick errors

Hopefully, it is obvious that while barometric measures do not change business to business, this list of diagnostic measures will vary as specific root causes within the goals are sought and determined in each specific situation. Diagnostic measurements in the context of data accuracy are problem-solving tools for determining what the root causes are for variation in accuracy.

The diagnostic measures are often generated from the measurement and root cause analysis process at the barometric level. For example, in the case of inventory location balance accuracy, a diagnostic metric could result as supplier counts are determined to be a root cause for inaccuracy of data. In the resolution phase of the analysis, there appropriately could be a diagnostic measurement of supplier count accuracy of parts received, compared to the receiving document. Diagnostic metrics are different at each organization depending on the causes for their variability, whereas the barometric measures are always the same regardless of product or process used in the converting or value-added process.

Inventory Location Balance Record Accuracy

The calculation is simple for determining the location balance record accuracy for Class A performance requirements. Normally, location balance counts are done as described in Chapter 9. Additionally, counts are done periodically in locations to confirm accuracy when suspicions arise. These and any other checks should also be included in the base for calculating accuracy. I have always referred to these counts as the "foul smell" counts. We count them because they are emitting a suspicious characteristic. The planning department is usually the one that gets the suspicious whiff first and requests the counts.

The calculation for inventory record accuracy is the total number of accurate location balances (allowing acceptable tolerances) divided by the number of location balances checked within that period.

$$\frac{\text{Total location balances accurate within tolerance}}{\text{Total location balances checked}} \times 100 = \text{Percent performance}$$

The tolerances noted in the numerator are the ABC stratification tolerances also discussed in the previous chapter on cycle counting.

Minimum Acceptable Class A Accuracy Standards

A items	±0 percent
B items	±2 percent
C items	±3 to 5 percent

There are no tolerances above 5 percent allowable in a Class A environment. The leeway from 3 to 5 percent is to allow inexpensive items such as pounds of inexpensive resin in a silo or washers worth $0.002 per piece to have a reasonable tolerance. The good news is that these more open tolerances are rarely required in today's high-performance organizations. Accuracy is allowed little tolerance if it can be discretely counted. If it can be counted, it can be accurate. Inventory weighing scales today are accurate enough that accuracy can be expected even on small parts.

> There are no tolerances allowed above 5 percent in high-performance organizations, and this is only allowed for D items and occasionally C items.

Each controlled area within the facility should be measured separately and the results posted visually for all employees to see. At the end of the week, these separate measures should be combined to calculate the overall facility inventory accuracy. This is done by increasing the total base in the metric calculation to include all locations counted. The numerator in the calculation will be the total locations that were counted and found to be correct throughout the facility. This allows everyone in the business to know globally how effective process control is in terms of inventory location balances and yet allow for individual understanding of each area's contribution prior to the consolidated performance view.

Class A ERP Performance

To reach Class A ERP levels of acceptance for inventory accuracy, the measurements are segmented into categories. Once the performance measurement is calculated, it can easily be translated into generally accepted worldwide ERP Class A standards.

- **95 to 100 percent, Class A performance** — Top management planning is in tact with solid linkage to the manufacturing and supply chain processes. Schedule adherence, data accuracy, and customer service are all at high levels of performance.
- **90 to 94 percent, Class B performance** — Planning processes are in place. Usually customer service is high, but there are still oppor-

tunities for low-hanging fruit for cost reduction. The supply chain may not be solidly linked to the management planning process.

- **80 to 89 percent, Class C performance** — Processes are loosely managed. Expediting is often the norm to support customer expectations. Top management is not engaged in the operations closely enough. Sales and operations have not accomplished a process handshake.

- **Below 80, failing process controls** — Management is negligent. If the company is successful, it is strictly because of a tolerant market. Data accuracy is not acknowledged as important and schedule adherence is coincidental when it happens. There is no operational competitive advantage in this position.

Class A

Class A performance is not equal to world-class performance. In most circles, it is a basis for process improvement, a foundation on which to build good process. It should be noted, however, that it is impossible to be a bad-performing organization and reach Class A standards. Class A means that, at least for basic processes, predictable high performance is reached and sustainable. These categories include:

1. Prioritization and management of business objectives
   - Project management
   - Human capital management and investment
   - Business imperatives
2. Sales and Operations Planning processes
3. Scheduling disciplines and production planning
4. Data integrity
5. Execution of schedules and plans

The metrics to accomplish the preliminary cut at Class A ERP include the following:

1. Sales and Operations Planning elements
2. Master production scheduling and rules of engagement disciplines
3. Materials planning
4. New product introduction
5. Procurement process

   6. First-time quality
   7. Shop floor management
   8. Safety
   9. Data accuracy
 10. Customer service
 11. Education and training

In a Class A environment, management is engaged and is monitoring the process through a predictable management system. Process owners are accountable to high standards and are expected to continue to improve performance over time.

Class B

Class B performance is where a lot of businesses jump off the improvement wagon. At 85 to 90 percent performance in the basic processes, predictability is reasonable in some managers' minds, and in many of these same businesses, there is not enough energy or commitment on management's part to break the last levels of inertia to get to Class A. Their sense of urgency is missing. The result is mediocre to good performance and lack of disciplined continuous improvement. Success relies heavily on the competition's tenacity for improvement. If it is an easy market, survival is likely.

Class C

Class C performance is nothing to brag about. Unfortunately, that is exactly where many businesses are when competition wakes them up. Class C businesses typically have management that thinks it is running and driving the business, but management's decisions are not always actually linked to business effect. Class C businesses only survive in markets with little competitive challenge. Class C businesses flounder in price-sensitive or customer-service-oriented markets.

Achieving Class A Certification

Class A is not a widely accepted standard in manufacturing. Unlike ISO, it has not had the sequence of events that led to its market drive. ISO had the European Community driving requirements as a mostly political answer to trade standards. It started off soft on substance and grew as subscribers raised their standards. Class A has had high standards from the start and they continue to grow. Ford Motor company introduced an MS9000 standard from the QS9000 standard that starts to address the high planning standards within Class A, but as of this writing has not been accepted globally. It is a mystery to me. Companies that have embraced it have become converts and often become passionate.

Glen Barton, CEO of Caterpillar, was the keynote speaker at the 2002 APICS International Conference in Nashville. It was enjoyable to hear him credit Class A and Six Sigma as two of the most important drivers of performance improvement in his company. With the performance of Caterpillar in terms of customer service and growth, that alone would be an adequate testimonial. Other well-known companies that have embraced this concept in the past are AlliedSignal (now Honeywell), Sweetheart Cup, NCR, Electrolux, Raymond Corporation, and hundreds of others.

Class A certification can be achieved from various consultant firms. DHSheldon & Associates has Class A as a major focus of process improvement. Others such as Oliver Wight Consulting and Buker, Inc. are also experts in this field.

The Weekly Performance Review

We have discussed the weekly performance review a few times in this book. It is worth detailing a little more. In high-performance organizations, there is always a performance review infrastructure sometimes referred to as a management system. In Class A ERP facilities, there is always a weekly performance review meeting, and it is held early in the week at the same time each week. The plant manager runs the meeting and process owners report the performance of their areas of responsibility for the previous week. These process owners should include all the metrics that have been named in this book and any others you can think of that will help your business meet its goals, and, of course, inventory location balance accuracy is one of them.

The reporting format for the weekly performance review meeting should be "institutionalized" for best process control. The quad chart in Chapter 9 is the right format.

The measurements reported at the weekly performance review meeting certainly do not have to be limited to the traditional Class A ERP measures. Metrics like inventory accuracy require supporting diagnostic measures to uncover the real root causes and should also be reported at this meeting by their prospective process owners. The quad report format works for any of these measures and should be a requirement for process ownership and reporting in the weekly performance review.

> **P**erformance measurement is the window on performance. Without it, there is no gauge for progress.

Performance measurement is the window on performance. Without it, there is no real way to gauge progress. High-performance teams measure all kinds of processes, not only to keep improving them, but also to indicate consistent quality of both product and data.

This book has free materials available for download from the Web Added Value™ Resource Center at www.jrosspub.com.

12

Bill of Material and Routing Record Accuracy Introduction

In addition to inventory location balance accuracy, it is essential to have accuracy in other records used to plan inventory flow and availability. Two such examples are bills of material and routing records. Although it is not the intention of this book to cover all aspects of data integrity requirements, it is proper to include a short discussion on these because they have such a big impact on planning material availability. These factors can also impact inventory accuracy.

Bill of Material Accuracy

Components

Bills of material (BOMs) are the recipes for the manufacturing process. They also are the records to drive proper assemblage of components for kits in a distribution environment. There are several components of accuracy in BOM records:

- Part number accuracy of parent level
- Part number accuracy of all components
- Unit of measure accuracy and consistency

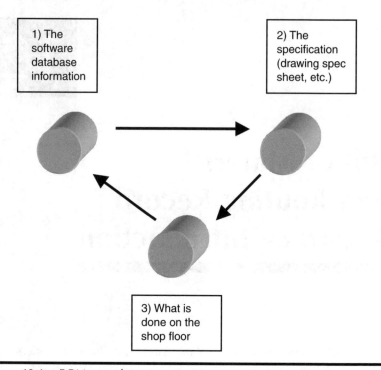

Figure 12-1. BOM record accuracy process.

- Quantity per part accuracy
- BOM structure as it compares to the actual process

The secret to a good accuracy process as it relates to BOM records is simple. There are three applications of BOM records and they all need to be in synchronization. They are:

1. What the computer record shows as the BOM
2. What the drawing or specification calls out as the BOM structure
3. What actually is done on the factory or warehouse floor (see Figure 12-1)

When all three of these files are matched, the result is an accurate BOM record that can be used to manage change in the product, flow inventory, and maintain predictable quality. BOM accuracy can be especially important if backflush transactions are used to impact inventory balance changes.

Process Owner

In most organizations, engineering is responsible for the design of products and for detailing specifications required of those products. The BOM is the production translation of this specification into manufacturing terms. This record is used to order and flow materials into place and to assemble the components or raw materials into usable/salable products. For this reason, engineering is usually the process owner for BOM accuracy.

> **E**ngineering typically owns the process for BOM accuracy. Engineering is responsible for designing and updating these records.

Some smaller organizations or companies that do not focus on new product introduction as a main core process do not have a separate R&D engineering department. In some cases, they might utilize manufacturing engineers or even production lead people to make some of the traditional engineering decisions. In these organizations, someone other than engineering must be designated as the BOM accuracy process owner.

In a process manufacturing environment where there is no product engineering group, typically the process or manufacturing support engineering group or person is the owner. Whoever has ultimate say on the product configuration as it relates to the recipe is the process owner.

One of the most often-heard responses from engineering on this topic is: "I (engineer) can be held responsible for the drawing and maybe even the computer record, but I can't control what the factory floor or warehouse clerk does." That may be true, but in reality, when specifications are not followed, engineering has little chance of succeeding. It is in the best interests of engineering to have its specifications followed. As engineering gets involved in the audit process, it often finds variation it has not been entirely aware of. This can even result in *higher* quality as engineering designs more manufacturability into the product. The bottom line? Engineering should be the process owner and audit and report performance at the weekly performance review.

When production deviates from specification, it should be noted, with actions resulting to eliminate this condition. When the computer is out of synchronization with the specification, again, accuracy performance should be reported, with resulting actions. While engineering is not always the one to do the fix, it can be the overseer. Everybody gains and most learn from the process focus.

Measuring BOM Accuracy

The threshold of acceptability for Class A performance in BOM accuracy is 99 percent accuracy. This means that 99 percent of the BOM records must be perfect.

It is not unusual to have several thousand BOM records on file within a manufacturing database. Many organizations have situations where a great majority of the product produced only uses about 20 percent of the part numbers. This can mean that a random sample in work in process would skew toward frequently used records simply because they are in the system more often. The majority of the high-usage parts will be verified quickly, and they have the potential to be selected randomly time and time again because of the frequency of use. This is obviously not a valuable use of resource once the accuracy is verified. The following are a few techniques that can be used, some of which deal with the issue of frequently used BOM records and the effect on the metric.

Random Sample

In a simple random method, a sample is done daily in released BOMs until both the confidence and verified accuracy are high. Usually this is done by production workers under the direction of the process owner for BOM accuracy (usually engineering). A random selection of assemblies might be chosen in the morning, and these orders (work orders, shop orders, pick tickets, etc.) are flagged for audit. Workers are trained to scrutinize these jobs for accuracy in all vital areas. A flag on the item master is logged for each BOM as it is checked for accuracy. This eliminates the chance of checking the same BOM too often.

Any error within the BOM makes that BOM inaccurate for the purpose of the measurement. If ten BOMs are checked and two have errors somewhere in the structure, the performance is reported as 80 percent.

Accuracy Deduction

In many environments, after checking BOMs for a few weeks, the accuracy is high enough that errors are not detected often through the daily random sampling. This may be a sign of verified BOM accuracy for released BOMs. At this time, it very well may be appropriate to move to another method of measurement. One is the accuracy deduction method. While some statisticians might get heartburn from it, it does its job.

When the normal audit method gets to the point that errors are seldom found, the performance is (appropriately) continuously reported at 100 percent. People start to lose any enthusiasm toward finding errors. In these same environments, occasionally there is still a "feeling" that 100 percent is not the right number because when new products are launched, there are often problems, and when nonfrequently made items are manufactured, there are often errors. This may be a good time to find and post errors as they are detected and stop the process of sampling BOMs on a daily basis. The question of how to measure this is still open.

In the accuracy deduction method, each error that is found is given a value of 2 percent and is subtracted from 100 percent. If there is one error, the performance for the day is 98 percent. If there are five errors, the performance is 90 percent and so on. A person with statistical tendencies reading this might be wringing their hands nervously after that measurement definition. Remember that the objective is not to post a number; the objective is high performance. When errors occur, it is better to have solid recognition of those errors. That forces reporting at the weekly performance review and root cause elimination.

Entire Database Sample

In make-to-stock (MTS) environments, often there are fewer end-item configurations. In these environments (with less than a few thousand BOM structures), it might make sense to sample the entire BOM database. Often there are very few obsolete BOMs maintained anyway, so it is in the best interests of high performance to cycle through the entire BOM record file. This can be done by item number order or it may make more sense to audit BOMs in the order of volume usage.

Some companies have hundreds of thousands of BOM records. These companies often utilize a make-to-order (MTO) or engineer-to-order (ETO) manufacturing methodology that drives the number of possibilities up tremendously. If you are in one of these environments, you may be asking the question: "How do these companies surface or segregate the right database for audit?" A suggestion is to create a firewall between the general database and the ones that are known to be probable manufacturing repeats.

Creating the Firewall

Many organizations have found that by creating a firewall between some of their data, they can greatly reduce the maintenance spending on data upkeep. The firewall is usually created by defining a "readiness code" field in the item master. Let us say that P is the readiness code designated for "production ready" records. For an item to meet readiness, it has to meet minimum criteria for accuracy.

A leading manufacturer of forklift trucks and other material handling equipment in the 1980s had over 150,000 BOM records. Some of these BOMs were not used frequently, but could be called up occasionally in "same as except for" applications. Businesses in MTO environments often find themselves in this situation. It makes little sense to audit these seldom (if ever) used BOMs or, in fact, to do any maintenance to these data. This company knew that to simply ignore these BOMs, without a supporting system for integrity of BOM structures, could have a disastrous result. What this company did was create a firewall to segregate its data, known from unknown.

In its environment, for an item to get a P (production ready or releasable) designation in the readiness code field on the item master, it had to meet the following rigid criteria as a minimum:

1. The record must have a complete and unique part number (not assigned to another item).
2. The record must have a cost standard loaded (even if it is estimated).
3. If it was a parent number (higher level in a BOM), a recorded audit reflecting latest revisions and part number changes had to be present and available.
4. If it was a manufactured item, an audited routing record reflecting current machine and work centers needed to be loaded. It should also reflect accurate lead times from the routing.
5. The record must include a stocking code indicating if it is a stocked item or an MTO component part.
6. The record should include a lead time if it is a purchased part.

By forcing these requirements for an item prior to allowing it to be released into production, all seldom-used items would have to be converted to a P status prior to release. In this example, a P also was an indicator that the item would have to be kept up to the latest revision for eternity each time an engineering change was authorized that in some way connected to this item number (unless the production-ready status was changed). This was a big benefit to this company because it was not acceptable in terms of maintenance costs for seldom-used parts or assemblies to be constantly maintained. The company's environment was one of constant, high-volume change activity.

Some organizations use additional codes in the same item master field for seldom-used items. In this example, let's define the production ready code on the item master as X. This will designate "one time only" (seldom) used parts. Like the P-coded item, an X item would have to meet all the criteria for release, but as soon as it is completed, it would again be treated as a nonmaintained item. Engineering change would not update this item until it was called into action again, if ever. In this example, the firewall procedure would stop any item *not* designated as a P from being released or ordered. Even an X item would have to be reviewed every time it was released. This saves on engineering maintenance and costs when items are often "one time only." Anything with a P status has to be maintained always and kept current through every engineering change connected to it. A non-P is behind the firewall and has to be reviewed each time (if) it is used in production.

This process allows engineering to invent and utilize the database any way it wants without any risks to production or inventory control. As long as engineering stays behind the firewall with its experimental BOM designs, they are not bothering anyone. Many organizations find this a rewarding system in more ways than one.

Routing Records Accuracy

Routing records are the process steps or maps that materials follow through the process of being converted from raw material into finished goods. Routing records can be very important in some organizations and not important at all in others, other than for cost standards.

In regulated organizations such as pharmaceuticals, the routing is important as a definition of process.

Routing records can be very important in some organizations and not important at all in others, other than for cost standards.

It has to be accurate and has to be followed to the letter due to government regulation and liability concerns. In these companies, a lot of attention is paid to routing records.

In traditional metal fabricating companies and long cycle time processes, routing accuracy is also important. Routing accuracy in these businesses must also be in the 99+ percent range. In these environments, raw material goes through several conversion operations and may travel reasonably long distances through the process. Here, routing records are necessary for the planning process. These routings might read something like:

Operation	Instruction	Machine Center
010	Saw to length	7230
020	Flamecut notch	7620
030	Deburr/grind	3410
040	Form	4620
999	Receive into stock	9999

These routings tend to support longer cycle times and more queue time as jobs move through functional departments such as "saw department" or "lathe area."

Today's high-performance organizations are opting for short cycle times where material travels only short distances and operations are close in proximity and batches are small. In these environments, the same routings might read something like:

Operation	Instruction	Cell
010	Make part	3
999	Move to cell 7	7

In these environments, no labor transactions are done because the time to do the process is extremely short. In these companies, only inventory transactions are recorded.

Reviewing the record accuracy of routings is done much like that of BOMs. Engineering, usually manufacturing engineering or processing engineering, is the responsible department and process owner for the accuracy audit and reporting. In smaller businesses where people wear many hats, again, someone from production would probably be the right person for this process ownership.

Many of the newer computer systems have combined the BOM record and the routing record into one integrated record file in the system. These are usually referred to as bills of resource (BORs). The BOM structure in this application is expanded to include the process in which the component part is used. Sequencing and timing can be better planned. Again, this is not as beneficial in process flow or lean environments where inventory moves fast through several processes.

Summary

In this chapter, we digressed slightly from pure inventory accuracy and looked briefly at the importance of BOMs and routing records as they relate to the item master in managing data. This is worth the time and effort, as the item master is the center of all activity in the manufacturing world. If it is important to manufacturing, it is linked to the item master. In the next chapter, we will look at this thought in detail and discuss the item master accuracy.

13

Item Master Record Accuracy Introduction

No other file is more important than the item master. In fact, the manufacturing world revolves around the part number, the focus and center of the item master file. All manufacturing records are attached to this file in some way. The item master is like the nucleus of the manufacturing database.

At the center of all manufacturing data lies the item master. You may have noticed that attached to each item number in the item master are several fields of data. These are the identifiers for all activity and knowledge associated with this part number. Many of these fields are required fields, such as standard cost, stocking code, or procurement code. A required field is generally linked or hard coded into the software logic and is necessary to use other functions properly. These required fields are especially important and should be utilized in the manner designed by the software provider.

All of the item master fields — required, nonrequired, and user definable — are included in your business system for data sorts and represent the keys to the real power of the system.

Other fields such as group code, family code, sales code, or planner code may not be required fields, but are very helpful in running a business in a cost-effective manner. Still other fields are user-defined fields. These are the fun fields in the item master. They are available for all the imaginative and creative process improvements you may want to implement. These fields are neither required nor labeled by the software originally. All of these fields — required, nonrequired, and user definable — are included in your business system for data sorts and represent the keys to the real power of the system. They are not to be taken lightly. This cannot be stressed enough!

Assigning Ownership of the Fields

Each of the fields in the item master should have ownership defined. The item master in its entirety does not belong to any one group or department within the company. It belongs to all groups. For example, organizations that use standard cost would want to have tight controls over the standard cost field as it can affect inventory valuation, the asset register, and even the income statement. The standard cost field should belong to the finance department. Only the finance department should be authorized to change that field. Finance becomes the process owner of that field of information and responsible for its accuracy. Many systems are even designed with security levels associated with fields, not screens. This allows others to look at any fields in the item master, but not to change them without authorization.

The materials department usually ends up owning the most fields in the item master, but even the sales department should have fields assigned for its use with the agreement that no one can change the information in the field except the owner. This gives each group or department the power to sort records and manipulate data. This allows creative problem solving to flourish. Fields of interest to the sales people might include family codes, customer codes, demand history, etc. Some of these might very well be user-defined fields because software business system suppliers do not usually detail the sales function as it can vary greatly from business to business in ways manufacturing does not.

Creating New Part Numbers

The engineering change control process should include the introduction of new part numbers. The "firewall" method described in Chapter 12 can work well with new item introduction. Engineers should be allowed to do whatever they want (within reason) with part number assignment. If they choose to assign several part numbers but later, prior to product launch, change the design and eliminate some of them — fine. If there is a firewall protecting production from inaccurate or incomplete information being released, it does not affect production. Having a procedure that stops any incomplete, nonproduction-ready information from being released creates a barrier between invention and production.

Auditing the Item Master Accuracy

Not all fields within the item master are critical to the planning of material availability and flow. Each organization will utilize the item master in its own way depending on the cycle time, number of markets served, and process flow. A responsible high-performance company usually has an item master accuracy procedure where specific fields of concern are audited regularly. The auditor of many of the more critical fields is often the company controller. His or her job is to choose a few fields randomly each week and check them for signs of proper maintenance. Each process owner will have to feed the controller with their definitions of accuracy. Some, like lead time, can be checked by creating reports that show history on the item.

Conclusion

There are many more topics concerning the item master that could be covered if this book were to do justice to the topic, but that is not the purpose of this book. It is a good idea to be aware that there are many other opportunities in the organization to aid in cost reduction through better, more accurate data.

14

A Word About Technology in the Inventory Accuracy Implementation

We have not said very much about technology to this point in the journey. Many people have strong opinions about this subject. I know this because I have heard them. Let us get this topic out of the way.

Technology has driven much of the real productivity gains in the world in recent years. Bar codes, radio frequency (RF) scanners, radio frequency identification devices (RFID), and automated material handling equipment are just a few of the technological advances that have affected the stores areas in our manufacturing facilities. In every case, these devices have improved the lives of the users and the integrity of the operation. But do not be fooled. Just as the manager who thinks that ERP software will deliver an ERP process is disappointed, so is the manager who relies on bar codes alone to solve the accuracy problems.

Any technology works well when people follow the process design. There are few applications where process technology is so foolproof that even exceptions are handled with ease. On the other hand, there are few processes without exceptions.

I have been in many warehouses where bar code scanners were sold internally as the answer to the accuracy problems. I would like a nickel for every time I have been told, "Oh, if we could just get the new scanners to read the bar code on the trucks, we wouldn't have these accuracy issues." Few usually believe me at first when I tell them that in most of the cases when scanners are installed without education and process disciplines implemented, the scanners do not deliver.

Just recently, I was in a high-volume assembly factory and the comment was made that its accuracy issue would be taken care of if there was an automated bar code scanner at the end of the line to read the boxes as they entered the warehouse. That immediately brought to mind a couple of other plants, one that was a sister facility to this one and another paper products manufacturer that had this exact hardware in place. Both of these other plants were brought to mind because they were in the exact position as this plant — inventory accuracy was lacking and costs were the result. Scanners alone can be overrated. I just smiled and waited for a better time to explain.

However, every once in a while, some process idea or technology really shakes up the marketplace. The reverse auction is one that did it for me. These Internet auctions seem to make an interesting difference in the marketplace. There are many success stories involving them. The essence of this practice goes against everything I learned and believed from my many years of experience. In some strange way, I wonder if RFID could be another one for me. After all, even though I have worked in the technology fields, I am still most passionate about process design, not the more flashy technology. RFID may change my mind.

RFID, I have to imagine, will bring a new wave of learning into the warehouse as it matures. Imagine each part having a broadcasting capability with receivers picking up and sorting the signals of each specific part in the warehouse. Suppose that each time a part crossed the painted line on the perimeter of the stores area, a deduction was made automatically to the balance by a receiver tracking the parts. That would mean, for example, that every time you brought your cart out of the grocery store, you would not have to stop at the checkout. The receiver at the door would log your purchases and charge your debit card.

Companies like NCR are developing this technology and retail giants like Wal-Mart are implementing and experimenting with it. It will happen in the future. At that time, I suppose a rewrite of this book will be necessary and technology will probably play a different role. For now, however, the parts still need to be transacted and the balances still are a requirement of good planning accuracy, so we are back to discipline as the cornerstone of success. Until we can buy discipline, we are stuck making it happen manually.

15

120 Days: 95+ Percent Inventory Balance Accuracy — The Big Celebration!

In the past 120 days, the organization has undergone some major changes in the way it works, thinks, and approaches accountability. It's time to reflect and celebrate! The rewards will come quickly to the organization, and people need to be thanked for their hard work and determination. ENJOY!

The Celebration

The final celebration should be significant when Class A levels of performance are reached. There has been a lot of dedication and determination to this point. Many organizations celebrate with a gala and music, food, and time off. Whatever method is chosen, it should involve everyone and, as appropriate, *feature* some of the most important players, the ones doing the transactions as well as the people doing the cycle counting and reconciliation. These are also usually the people who did and will continue to do the training.

This final celebration of Class A inventory record accuracy should be recognizably different than previous celebrations. People should know this is a significant company-wide achievement. The CEO should be involved and address the workforce in its entirety in some appropriate way. This can be through a video address played to all departments, as has been done in some companies, or in face-to-face meetings with departments or plants. Certainly the warehouse people and the production people involved in the implementation need to be praised. Bottom-line results/payback should be communicated and stressed.

> Now the challenge is to keep the processes in control.

Now the challenge is to keep the processes in control. It will take just as much determination and management involvement to sustain the process. It must remain a top priority in the organization.

Data Accuracy Summary

Data accuracy is critically important for predictable high-performance results. All businesses, whether in manufacturing, distribution, retail, banking, or service industries, have to have predictable data to make quick accurate decisions. Since the speed of processes and quickness in meeting or defining market need is playing a more and more important part in being competitive, accuracy is even more important.

Many departments or segments within planning and process improvement in an organization involve some outside factors not fully within their control at all times. Customers, for example, usually play that role. We all know that the inability to forecast customer needs and expectations 100 percent accurately often plays a part in the variability of the manufacturing process, but we generally also acknowledge that this will never be perfect.

Record accuracy is not the same discussion as forecasting accuracy. Record accuracy has much less to do with outside forces. The good thing about record accuracy, especially inventory record accuracy, is that no one outside the organization is needed to complete this job successfully. Everything that is required to achieve 95+ percent location balance accuracy resides internally. Serious organizations get this job done in 120 days or less. God bless!

Glossary of Terms

ABC Stratification — The stratification of inventory into levels associated with monetary and/or volume levels. Materials planning utilizes this methodology extensively in planning methodologies.

APICS — American Production and Inventory Control Society. This organization of professionals is the keeper of the body of knowledge for inventory planning topics and process flow materials. APICS can be reached at 1-800-444-APIC.

ATO (Assemble to Order) — An inventory strategy that master schedules assemble for availability when demand happens. Subassemblies and/or components are assembled after the demand signal. Dell Computer has made this strategy famous in recent years.

Audit — To audit a process such as inventory accuracy is to check accuracy of a process by a defined periodic check and measure.

Auto-Transactions — Same as backflushing.

Backflushing — A method of auto-deducting inventory balances from triggers created at transaction times such as the completion of production or the receipt transaction of inventory into finished goods.

Balance by Location — An inventory balance for only one location where a material or item is stored. This should not be confused with having more than one item in a location. They do not address the same subject.

Batch Environment — The process where transactions are not processed in the system at the time the actual event took place. Records of the transactions are kept and batched until they are entered into the computer system at a later time, usually at shift end or end of day. This is not a widely used system today because faster systems are widely available.

BOM (Bill of Material) — A record file that documents the description of all component and ingredient relationships including "quantity per" and all item and material numbers. It normally resides in the computer business system, but copies may also be available in the engineering design systems.

BOR (Bill of Resource) — A record file that documents the bill of material information along with the routing records. It documents the sequence of materials used in the process by tying each component to a process step.

Brainstorming — A technique used to develop ideas in a problem-solving effort. Team members take turns submitting ideas that are documented for later review.

Buker, Inc. — A consulting organization in Chicago that is involved in ERP education and training including video offerings (www.Buker.com).

Business Imperatives — The shorter term business objectives that *must be done* in the next twelve months for competitive advantage as determined by top management. Not to be confused with strategic objectives, which are longer term.

Business System — A computer system used to communicate linkages between processes such as scheduling and execution of schedules, inventory consumption and balance records, forecasting and planning inventory, financials and operations, etc. Business systems are usually referred to as ERP systems.

Carousels — Moving racks that carry material to the pickers as opposed to traditional racks where forklifts carry the pickers to the inventory. Carousels are normally linked to the business system, which allows automation and efficiency of the picking operation.

Class A ERP — A specific high level of performance using ERP methodology and defined by measurements and certification criteria. There are organizations (such as DHSheldon & Associates) that certify this performance level by auditing performance. The metrics are usually around five areas: prioritization and management of business objectives (includes project management, human capital management, and investment and business imperatives), Sales and Operations Planning processes, scheduling disciplines and production planning, data integrity, and execution of schedules and plans.

Consultants — Experts hired from outside an organization to aid in the implementation of an improvement process. Often education and training are a good application for consultants.

Control Group — A sample of items used for controlled counts and to determine root cause of errors in inventory balance accuracy.

Controlled Area — In inventory control terms, a controlled area is a defined area where inventory is kept, with procedures governing the issue and receipt of material flow, in and out. Usually this is an area that is (by process design or habit) meant to house the specific inventory for more than twenty-four hours.

Cumulative Lead Time — The summary of all lead time required to requisition material and convert this material into saleable inventory. Normal sequences include procurement, fabrication, subassembly, assembly, test, and ship.

Cycle Count — A cycle count program is designed to schedule and periodically audit inventory balances for accuracy. Normally, it is done using random sampling with a plan to count certain segments completely over specific periods of time. There can be wide variation in cycle counting programs depending on the process control in that particular stores area.

Demand Planning — Top management planning processes include demand planning. Demand planning is the process that results in the forecast of customer behaviors as they relate to the product sales of a business. Inputs to demand planning are normally business planning goals, marketing plans, sales cycle knowledge, customer knowledge, and history of seasonality and cyclicality.

DHSheldon & Associates — Consulting company involved with ERP education and training including inventory accuracy. Donald Sheldon is the author of this book and is president of DHSheldon & Associates.

Discipline — In inventory control and manufacturing environments, discipline normally refers to the action controls required for predictability or repeatability of a process. Processes need good disciplines or controls for repeatability.

Discrete Items — This term as used in inventory control means that items can be counted. Resin in a silo would not normally be considered a discrete item. Motors in a pallet would be considered discrete items.

ECN (Engineering Change Number) — Describes the serial number of a change as it is being completed and after it is completed. This is sometimes called an ECO (engineering change order).

ECO (Engineering Change Order) — Same as an ECN.

ECR (Engineering Change Request) — Usually the prerequisite to the ECN. This is the process and document used to suggest a change to a product. An ECR is not an authorized change.

End Items — Finished goods ready to ship. This refers to product in both make-to-stock and make-to-order environments.

ERP (Enterprise Resource Planning) — A methodology of linking and measuring business processes for the objective of high performance and low cost. Emphasis is on capacity and realities of process. Evolved from the MRP II process methodology, ERP added more emphasis on linkages outside the business (suppliers and customers). Sometimes referred to as supply chain management.

ETO (Engineer to Order) — A methodology used in manufacturing when the demand signal has some of the necessary information to complete a product properly. The manufacturing process is not started until the customer has ordered the item, which signals engineering to spec the job.

Finished Goods — Inventory that is customer ready and could be sold and delivered in the time it takes to pack and ship the product.

Fishbone Analysis — A method or tool for problem solving using a fishbone diagram and process. Usually the factors considered include variation sources from the following: methods used in the process, machinery or equipment required, manpower or people factors, materials, and environmental issues.

5-Why Diagram — Problem-solving process for breaking bigger problems into smaller components and determining causes.

Forecasting — The process deliverable from top management demand planning. The forecast is designed to predict customer behaviors, taking into consideration both history and actions to affect that behavior. In high-performance businesses, it is updated and reviewed at least monthly and more recently it is often reviewed weekly.

Golden Zoning — The arrangement of inventory locations to help efficiencies of picking or to support ergonomics of the pickers.

Inventory — Material, components, or finished goods held for or used in the process of manufacturing or distribution.

Inventory Control — Involves the process of storing, moving, and managing the inventory of an organization. Elements include managing obsolescence, accuracy, availability, and general levels of inventory.

Inventory Record — A computer system record that shows the quantity of on-hand inventory of any specific item or material.

Inventory Stratification — The stratification of inventory into levels associated with monetary and/or volume levels. Materials planning utilizes this methodology extensively in planning methodologies. See ABC Stratification.

Ishikawa Diagram — Cause-and-effect problem-solving tool using a fishbone diagram and process.

Item Master Record — The "master" record by part number within the computer system where vital information linked to that item or material is kept.

JIT (Just in Time) — Same as lean manufacturing.

Lean Manufacturing — Focuses on eliminating waste or cost-added activities in all processes in a business. Objectives of lean drive flexibility and speed of process.

Location — Labeled area where inventory can be or is held. The location description is also sometimes referred to as the location.

Master Scheduler — Directs the development and execution of the master schedule. He or she helps direct the "rules of engagement" between the demand signal and the supply-side delivery process.

Master Scheduling — The process of linking demand and top management planning processes to the factories or procurement of a manufacturing or distribution business. The master schedule creates the drumbeat for the supply chain and gives specific direction on both planned and unplanned schedule requirements.

Material Issue — The transaction that decreases an on-hand inventory balance.

Material Receipt — The transaction that increases an on-hand inventory balance.

Materials Management — The functional group responsible for scheduling, planning, procuring, and controlling inventory in a manufacturing organization. In some manufacturing organizations, procurement is in a separate functional group.

MPS (Master Production Schedule) — The process by which all product is scheduled through a factory or distribution facility. It normally drives requirement signals into the planning process and sets the drumbeat for the future requirements.

MRP (Material Requirements Planning) — A subprocess of ERP that nets available and scheduled inventory against requirements from the master schedule. In most companies today, this process is done in some form for materials planning in future time buckets.

MRP II (Manufacturing Resource Planning) — The predecessor to ERP. MRP II was a business planning system in the 1980s and 1990s that integrated capacity planning and top management planning with the materials planning and plan execution. It was changed into ERP in the 1990s with the integration of supply chain management.

MTO (Make to Order) — When organizations plan subcomponents prior to the customer demand signal and finish manufacturing the product after the customer order, it is referred to as an MTO environment. MTO is usually referred to as an inventory strategy.

MTS (Make to Stock) — When organizations plan and build finished-level inventory prior to the customer demand signal, it is referred to as an MTS environment. MTS is usually referred to as an inventory strategy.

Obsolescence — High-performance companies define this as the point at which inventory is no longer expected to be used in any reasonable time frame. Usually, inventory that is not planned to be used in the next two years or more would be considered obsolete. This often becomes an issue when engineering change orphans a part due to a replacement design.

Oliver Wight — Consulting company involved with ERP education and training including inventory accuracy.

Pareto Chart — Frequency chart of root causes. In this case, it refers to the root cause of inventory inaccuracies.

Physical Inventory — Also referred to often as the "wall-to-wall physical," this is the process of occasionally counting all inventory in a section or whole facility or organization.

POU (Point-of-Use) Inventory — A stores method where inventory is held at the area it will be consumed, such as in welding or in assembly. POU inventory can be tracked financially as part of work-in-process inventory or it can be stores inventory not held in a traditional centralized stores area.

Primary Locations — Permanent locations established by SKU (stockkeeping unit). As SKUs are received into the storage area, they are put away in existing assigned locations. Primary location design is the opposite of random location system design.

Procurement — The purchasing function within an organization responsible for procuring items required by the company. Responsibilities usually include contract negotiations, supplier selection, pricing, reverse auctions, and supplier performance.

Random Locations — When warehouses utilize random locations, put-away of newly received product is always into empty locations. The opposite of a random location process is the primary location process design.

Receipt or Material Receipt — The transaction that increases an on-hand inventory balance.

Repetitive Manufacturing — An environment where the same items are often repeated. System shortcuts can make sense, and many business systems are set up specifically to accommodate this type of efficiency.

Reverse Auction — A process in which suppliers are asked to bid on specifications and pricing for services and/or components against other suppliers in an open Internet auction. It is referred to as "reverse" because the bidding goes down during the auction, not up.

Routing — See Routing Record.

Routing Record — Documented description of the process steps used in manufacturing or converting raw material and/or components into finished and semi-finished goods.

Strategic Objectives — Longer term goals for an organization. These goals tend to define the priorities and outline top management expectations going forward. The time frame is usually in the two- to five-year range.

Stratification — See Inventory Stratification.

Tolerance — APICS allows and has documented acceptable inventory accuracy tolerances (A = ±0 percent, B = ±2 percent, C = ±3 to 5 percent). These tolerances are allowed for less expensive parts for efficiency.

Transaction — A specific record of a financial, inventory, or labor action. These are normally captured in business system records and are accessible by auditors and control personnel. In inventory accuracy efforts, transactions are the records of inventory movement including receipts and issues to inventory balances.

"24-Hour" Rule — When inventory is stored in an area (by process design or normal habit) for more than twenty-four hours, it falls into this rule. In this situation, it is generally considered responsible to know where this inventory is by tracking it in the business system. Inventory that is held less than twenty-four hours in any one area often is tracked at the next twenty-four-hour point or at finished goods.

Wall-to-Wall Physical Inventory — Same as a physical inventory.

WIP (Work in Process) — Inventory that has been issued or charged to the manufacturing process. Examples include component inventory as it is charged out to the factory at the time of kitting.

Work Order — Used in some businesses to define a specific job requirement with configuration requirements and quantity required. In a repetitive environment, work orders are often not used.

Gantt Chart of the Inventory Record Accuracy Project Plan

The outline on the next few pages can be used for your actual Gantt chart (see Figure A-1). It should be helpful. The project plan has been summarized with typical timing.

Day 1–3: Preparing for Inventory Record Accuracy

People in the business need to understand the reasons behind the effort required to achieve Class A performance levels in inventory location balance records. Step one is education. The source of this education can be from outside experts, canned video education, detail courses, APICS, etc. This may be the most important step as you prepare for high-performance inventory accuracy.

Day 4: Discovering Transactions and Inventory Flow

Once the education is started, the next step of understanding the existing process can begin. This step normally begins with the acknowledgment of inventory flow through the plant or facility. Map the entire flow through the process and define the controlled areas (inventory that is held in an area for more than twenty-four hours) and where inventory normally is stored.

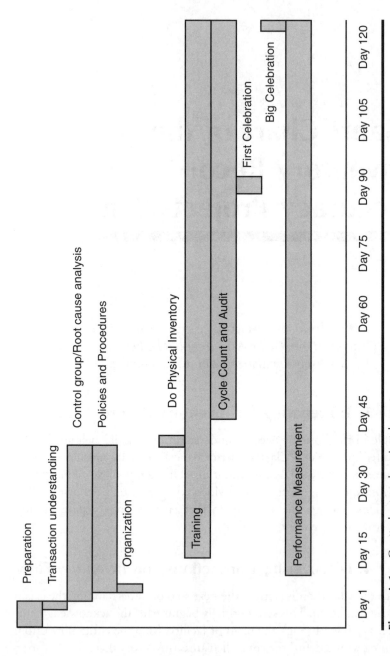

Figure A-1. Gantt chart and project layout.

Determine the transactions that are done today and the transactions that should be done to best serve the needs of accuracy. The next sequential step is to list the people who do these transactions and then compare that to a list of people certified to do these specific transactions. Actions should result from this exercise.

Day 5–45: Control Group and Root Cause Analysis

By day 5, it should be time to start the control group. The objective of the control group is to determine the barriers or root causes limiting accuracy performance. Often there are but a few reasons once the facts are uncovered. Once a control group is successfully checked error-free for ten days in a row, initiate a second control group. This will be a powerful exercise and much will be learned.

Days 8–45: Policies and Standard Operating Procedures, The Training Tools for Process Control

As soon as the transactions are defined and the controlled areas are documented, it is time to begin the documentation of transaction procedures. This will not be completed in just a couple of days; it will be an ongoing process. The procedures will be refined as the root cause of error is determined. Nonetheless, the documentation should begin because of the learning and improvement that will result. These documents are also needed for the training.

Day 9: Inventory Organization and Storage Patterns

By the ninth day, it will start to become obvious that improvements in the organization of inventory are necessary. The mapping will say so, and the control group will confirm it. At this time, a blueprint should be detailed and reviewed defining the flow and determining improvements that would control the transaction processes. By the way, this does not normally include fences in high-performance organizations.

Day 15 and Beyond: Training for Process Control

Training can now begin. People have defined the inventory control process and procedure documentation is started. The first to be trained are the warehouse employees and material handlers. The procedures are the training guides. Proper use of performance measurement and root cause analysis should also be part of the training.

Day 35: Conduct the Last Wall-to-Wall Physical Inventory

At this point, the root causes of errors are understood and have, for the most part, been eliminated. This does not mean that the inventory stores areas are accurate. Too many errors from prior practices lurk there. At this point, a physical inventory will help clean most of this up (although not all of it).

Day 45: Cycle Counting and Auditing Process Control

The control group has identified the errors being committed. Once the processes are under control and the physical inventory has been completed, it is time to convert to a traditional cycle count process. This requires setting practices around frequency and rules on stratification of inventory.

Day 90: Celebration!

By day 90, processes should be in control and the last-ever physical inventory completed. Performance should be 90+ percent and the work done to this point deserves recognition. Celebration is part of education and teaches people the priorities of the organization more clearly.

Day 120: The Big Celebration

Shortly after reaching the 90 percent range, 95 percent will follow. The determination should not stop at 95 percent, but instead should get even more aggressive toward higher levels of performance. Celebrations should come each time a milestone is maintained. The next likely targeted milestone is 98 percent. Godspeed!

INDEX